Spirituality and Growth
on the Leadership Path

Spirituality and Growth on the Leadership Path

An Abecedary

DEBORAH J. HAYNES

Artwork by Michael Shernick

PICKWICK *Publications* · Eugene, Oregon

SPIRITUALITY AND GROWTH ON THE LEADERSHIP PATH
An Abecedary

Pickwick Publications
An Imprint of Wipf and Stock Publishers
199 W. 8th Ave., Suite 3
Eugene, OR 97401

www.wipfandstock.com

ISBN 13: 978-1-62032-227-7

Cataloguing-in-Publication data:

Haynes, Deborah J.

    Spirituality and growth on the leadership path : an abecedary / Deborah J. Haynes ; with artwork by Michael Shernick.

    xvi + 100 pp. ; 23 cm. Includes bibliographical references and index.

    ISBN 13: 978-1-62032-227-7

    1. Leadership. 2. Management. 3. Organizational effectiveness. 4. Spirituality. I. Shernick, Michael. II. Title.

HM1261 H39 2012

Manufactured in the U.S.A.

For those who aspire to lead
and in appreciation for those who have gone before

Contents

Contents

Acknowledgments

I OFFER MY GRATITUDE first to Michael Shernick, whose initial excitement about creating imaginative botanical illustrations for this book has come to fruition in the volume you now hold.

This *Abecedary* was inspired by many sources, including the natural world, poetry, and individuals in leadership positions. I mention nature first, because every day in the world provides revelations that influence both present joys and my sense of future possibilities.

The inspiration to read poetry, and to try my hand at writing it, comes from the mother-line in my family, especially my mother Mary Elizabeth Clark Haynes (1925–2005), whose library contained treasures that I mined as a young girl. My sister Catherine, a wise and gifted therapist, has shared many poems over the years, from W. B. Yeats to Wendell Berry, May Sarton to Mary Oliver. I found my own way to the ancients such as Herakleitus and to Russian poetic traditions, where Marina Tsvetaeva took my heart. Reading Japanese haiku of Basho, Issa, and others has motivated me to try to find images that express succinctly what my discursive mind would take volumes to tell. Many poets, living and dead, have furthered my poetic passion, but here I would mention M. C. Richards (1915–1999), Olga Broumas, Norman Weinstein, Gary Snyder, and Jane Hirshfield, each of whose work occupies a unique place in my consciousness.

Among individuals within the academy, I thank Dr. John Pierce, my first academic dean; Dr. Gretchen Bataille, the first provost with whom I had genuine dialogue; and Dr. Elizabeth Hoffman, the first university president whom I got to know as she demonstrated what indefatigable energy really means. College Deans Peter Spear and Todd Gleeson led with unusual grace. Associate Dean Merrill Lessley was an incredibly skilled dialogue partner. At other moments, Associate Deans Graham Oddie and Darna L. Dufour showed me the space between intelligent leadership and friendship. I learned about styles of leadership from more distant observation of Provost and Chancellor Phil DiStefano at the University of Colorado;

Acknowledgments

Dr. Wilson Yates, former President of United Theological Seminary; Bob James, former Fine Arts department head for decades at the University of Oregon; and Dr. Margaret R. Miles, former Academic Dean at the Graduate Theological Union. Over many years, I worked closely with exceptional individuals who taught me how to lead, and serve. Here I would mention Valerie Albicker, Alexei Bogdanov, Mildred Burgermeister, Shelley Dahme, Erika Doss, Linda Finfrock, Terry Greenberg, Linda Kerr-Saville, Del Kyhn, Sarah Matsuda, Sue Middleton, Elaine Paul, Lia Mir Pileggi, Rick Seydel, Michael Shernick, Lisa Tamaris Becker, and William Rumley.

In nonprofit organizations, I owe special debts to Michael Jones, Diane Jones, Kim Mooney, Sarah Varick, Bev Kronisch, Denise Hmieleski, Julie Thomas, and Reta Morrisette, as well as the dedicated staff in several Planned Parenthood offices around the country.

Many other individuals helped to nurture my leadership aspirations and hone my skills. I watched my mother struggle with unfulfilled ambitions throughout her life, while my father worked his way up the corporate ladder to become vice president of an international corporation. My sisters—Ann Cecile Thomas, Marie Christine Cannon, and Catherine Mary Haynes—supported me at every step. My son Mitchell Pearce is a corporate leader in his own right. And my husband David Thorndike has observed my process over nearly thirty years, heard my stories, and queried me often about my interpretation of events. Among many mentors on my leadership path, I must mention Sharon Campbell, with whom I spoke repeatedly about my aspirations and how they related to actual experience.

Special thanks to those who read chapters of this book and offered their feedback, including Mark Amerika, Lanny DeVono, Darna Dufour, John Frazee, Todd Gleeson, Catherine Haynes, Betsy Hoffman, Elvira Henson, Merrill Lessley, Bev Murrow, Hank Murrow, Margaret R. Miles, Elaine Paul, John Pierce, Andrea Rubin, Peter Spear, Tom Sebok, and Judith Thorpe.

In the literary production of this book, I offer gratitude in particular to award-winning editor Melanie Mulhall (http://www.DragonheartWritingandEditing.com), whose suggestions to me were both brilliant and practical. Helena Mariposa (http://www.ebooktransformation.com/) provided excellent assistance near the end of the writing process. The staff at Wipf and Stock—K. C. Hanson, Christian Amondson, Diane Farley, and Patrick Harrison—were absolutely superb to work with, and I appreciate this second opportunity to publish with them.

Finally, I am most grateful to my spiritual teachers, especially B. K. S. Iyengar, Angela Farmer, Victor Van Kooten, Felicity Green, Pema Chödrön, Larry Rosenberg, the Venerable Dzigar Kongtrül Rinpoche, and to the Mangala Shri Bhuti sangha, whose dedication to Buddhist practice and to collaborative leadership is a powerful inspiration.

Preface

THE TITLE OF THIS book is meant to elicit curiosity. What, you may ask, is "abecedary"? What does spirituality have to do with leadership? And how is leadership a path? While the book as a whole will answer each of these questions, here, at the outset, I offer an orientation to what follows.

The word abecedary is derived from the Latin *abecedarium*, alphabet or primer, and refers to a book arranged in alphabetical order. This is the book's structure.

Spirituality is a fuzzy term with vast implications across cultures and history. The term points toward the beyond, however we conceive it, and to our deepest core values. The world's wisdom traditions—philosophy and religion, mysticism and theology, including indigenous beliefs and rituals—are rich resources for reconceptualizing leadership. Although I do not purport to be an expert, I draw on these reserves of wisdom.

The book does not presume a particular religious or secular orientation, but is pertinent for people in a range of leadership roles across institutions, from universities to seminaries, from nonprofit organizations to businesses. It is designed to be relevant to any organization where one is called to a position of leadership. This *Abecedary* is meant to provide inspiration, a book that might be kept on one's desk during the course of a day, opened at random or opened as a particularly hot topic arises. Metaphors of growth are interwoven throughout these pages, with creative botanical illustrations by artist Michael Shernick.

At its foundation, the book asks you to undertake the inner work that can provide a compass for navigating the mundane affairs related to administration and management. I believe that leadership is a *path*, a *way* in the Taoist sense—a way to move, literally, but also a way of life. Some of us take this path as a duty, an institutional obligation, because we believe it is our turn. Often, we enter our first leadership position simply because we have been asked to take the job or our peers have elected us. Some see leadership as a path to power, self-affirmation, or self-aggrandizement. Some see it as a vocation, a true calling through which to serve others.

This last reason applies to my own leadership path. My formal academic degrees—BFA and MFA in visual arts from the University of Oregon, MTS from Harvard Divinity School, and PhD in the Study of Religion and Fine Arts from Harvard University—did not direct me specifically toward this path, but offered me opportunities to develop both my creative and scholarly life. I have worked for community and nonprofit groups for more than thirty years, and for nearly fifteen of those years served as a department chair or program director in two universities.

I participated in political activity during presidential campaigns and worked in the US on issues surrounding peace and justice in Central America and South Africa. I spent many years educating myself about nuclear disarmament, as well as reproductive freedom and choice, then served on boards of directors in those two arenas. In 2006–2007, I undertook more than eighty hours of training related to death and dying, and then began to work within our largest local hospice as a volunteer.

My first academic position was as director of a small women's studies program with approximately fifty undergraduate majors. Then, for four years, I chaired a large department of art and art history with nearly 1000 undergraduate and graduate students. Subsequently, I founded and directed a residential academic program in the visual and performing arts for eight years.

Over these years, I took advantage of opportunities to learn about leadership and management in many ways: through participating in an ongoing forum on women and leadership and a yearlong seminar for emerging leaders; by attending meetings and conferences; and by taking a forty-hour mediation training. Besides the mundane daily activities of my roles in higher education—budget management, curriculum development, staff hiring and supervision, faculty and student support, and conflict resolution—I responded to the unexpected. I labored on issues related to safety, including asbestos mitigation and intractable ventilation problems in an old building. I also began the planning for a new building, with ancillary activities of donor cultivation and fundraising that eventually led to a beautiful $63,500,000 facility—more than a decade and two department chairs later.

I have, in short, served in various capacities in both nonprofit and higher education worlds. Many fine administrators and leaders taught me a lot. Reading articles and books helped me to understand what I was experiencing. Being active in two Unitarian-Universalist churches and several Buddhist communities has helped to ground all of this service.

For years I kept a large binder with notes about workshops I attended and meetings with deans and faculty ombuds, articles about conflict resolution, reflections about how to work with challenging colleagues, and other useful information. I then compiled a version of this three-ring binder for my successor as department chairperson, presenting what I had learned about leadership and management. But I don't think it was ever opened, for I found it years later on a dusty back-corner bookshelf.

During the last decade, when asked to address emerging leaders, I would hand out "ABCs for Administrators," a succinct one-page set of imperatives with lessons that I had learned. Later, when our old and unsafe building was about to be demolished, I put up an exhibition in the department chair's office with over one hundred pages from the binder stapled to the wall. But the book you hold in your hand is clearly not a hefty three-inch-thick single-spaced set of documents with long reflections about leading, administering, and managing an organization. Instead, it contains the *pith instructions* about what I have learned: simple practical advice about the process and path of leadership.

This primer focuses on lessons that no one ever explicitly taught me, lessons that I have learned through my experience. Some topics are prosaic and mundane, dealing with ordinary everyday activities. My bookshelves are crowded with resources on practical topics related to my professional career, books on teaching, administration, consensus building, advocacy, and mediation. But few of these resources attend to the inner life of a person in a leadership position. Therefore, many of this book's themes are related to the inner moral and spiritual life. Besides incorporating illustrations, the book includes entries from what I call the "chronicles of experience," etymology and poetry, examples of contemplative practice and meditation, and metaphoric digressions for the engaged reader. There are common elements—lists and advice—and also uncommon elements, including recipes. Some of the chapters are short, as befits the topic, while others are longer.

The poet Carl Sandburg reputedly once said that "artist" is a praise word, not to be taken for oneself, but designated by a community to the one who creates. Perhaps "leader" is also such a praise word, an appellation for those who are elected or appointed by their peers to serve a particular community, and who serve well. I hope that *Spirituality and Growth on the Leadership Path: An Abecedary* will provide inspiration and insight as you navigate the shoals, deep water, rocky coasts, wind, and sunny climes of your own journey. May the blue sky serve as a metaphor for the clarity you seek to find on this path.

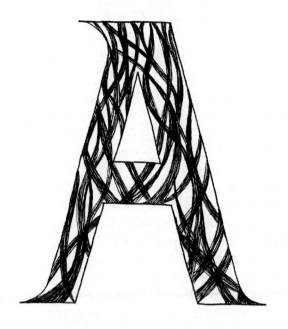

Administrator

The verb "administer" is related to *minister*,
from the French "servant." What might it mean to say
that an administrator is, first of all, a servant?

WHEN I ENCOUNTERED Robert K. Greenleaf's essays, collected in his 1977 book *Servant Leadership*, I found a provocative concept that helped me to reframe my aspiration and experience as an administrator in several contexts, including nonprofit organizations and institutions of higher education. In Greenleaf's view, a leader must be a servant first, one who wants to serve others and ensure that their needs are being met. The success of this process is measured by whether those who are being served become healthier, wiser, and more likely to become servants themselves. Grounded in altruistic values and a vision of community, such an administrator must follow an internal calling or vocation. Leadership in this model is not about personal gain and relentless pursuit of one's own self-interest. In fact, working for the common good means subordinating one's ego for higher goals. Yes, such an administrator has ambition, but this is channeled for the community one serves, not for the self.

Certainly, serving as a leader in any context has rewards. The rewards of my own service include: developing my leadership and management skills; exercising my vision; seeing my departments and programs grow and change; experiencing the fruits of my labor within the wider university and community; mentoring others and sharing their challenges and successes; helping to hire a new generation of staff and faculty and coordinating the activity of volunteers; collaborating with skilled personnel to run the programs; and participating in variety of non-routine projects such as fundraising and planning for new facilities.

But being an administrator also involves a tremendous amount of mundane activity. Here, at the beginning of this discussion on leadership, I want to emphasize prosaic ways of being, for they provide a way of thinking that foregrounds the everyday and ordinary. In a short essay, published as *Toward a Philosophy of the Act*, the Russian philosopher Mikhail Bakhtin emphasized that wholeness and integrity of the self are not given. Rather, they are always a matter of work, a project to be undertaken in daily life. "Every thought of mine," he wrote, "is an act or deed that I perform—my own individually answerable act or deed. It is one of all those acts which make up my whole . . . life as an uninterrupted performing of acts. For my entire life as a whole can be considered as a single complex act or deed that I perform . . ."[1] To speak of the commonplace, therefore, is a way of indicating that creating an integrated life takes a lifetime. Although this work may never be completed, it is nonetheless a responsibility that we carry out in daily life.

I have learned on the ground and in the trenches that the everyday activities of administration, both mundane and exotic, involve being comfortable with who I am, unafraid of being vulnerable, but also unafraid of the risks associated with taking a stand. For the administrator—and for anyone wanting to live a good life—nothing is more essential than authenticity and integrity.

Beginnings

With what values at the forefront of your
awareness will you begin?

I HAVE LOVED T. S. Eliot's poetry since I was a teenager. I read it silently in my mother's library and recited particular poems for an audience during competitions as a teen. I still relish the first line of "East Coker," part of Eliot's *Four Quartets*, in which he links the beginning of an activity, or even of a life, to its end. At the conclusion of this quartet, the conundrum of the last line always causes me to reflect, for there Eliot connects the end to the beginning.

I sought out mentors when I began my first administrative position, and this is a practice I highly recommend. My first dean, John Pierce, urged me to think about what I wanted my legacy to be—my end, in Eliot's sense. "What do you want to see when you look back?" he asked.

I did not answer immediately with the first thing that came to mind, but I have reflected about this in the years since that conversation. What I want is to look back on how my actions expressed my core values: kindness and compassion, humility and patience, discipline and generosity, modesty and accountability, moral courage and willingness to take risks, respect and open-mindedness. From where I stand today, I can say that my commitment to hold and communicate these values in my interactions has been strong and steady. Have I always succeeded? Of course not, but aspiration and intention set a stage for playing out the roles we must assume. A leader may leave one organization and move to another. Looking back as she leaves may well impact the beginning—and all the days that follow—in the next position.

When composing their poetry, modernist poets such as T. S. Eliot looked back, too, toward the wisdom of pre-Socratic philosophers, including Herakleitos. Of the many fragments attributed to him, translators differ in both the numbering of the fragments and their rendition of the original Greek.[2] In 1889, for example, G. W. T Patrick translated Fragment 70, "The beginning and end are common." In his 1954 scholarly study, G. S. Kirk offered a longer version: "But there is no such thing as a start and finish of the whole circumference of a circle: for every point one can think of is a beginning and end." Two more recent translations are more poetic to my ear. Guy Davenport's 1979 version simplifies the sentence: "The beginning of a circle is also its end." Brooks Haxton's "The beginning is the end" captures the essence of the meaning of Herakleitos's insight, and take us right back to Eliot. Every end is also a beginning.

What do *you* want to see when you look back?

FROM THE CHRONICLES OF EXPERIENCE

I vividly remember the day I accepted my second administrative position, as chair of an academic department at a large research university. Walking home from work on an early spring afternoon, I contemplated my choices: to stay where I was or accept the proffered position. I crossed the pasture where a neighbor kept horses, carefully avoiding the mare with her nursing filly. Rain clouds had just passed through, leaving my garden damp.

Kneeling to examine the vigorous garlic greens, I glanced up to see a fully articulated double rainbow that extended from horizon to horizon. This seemed like an auspicious sign, and I took it as support for accepting the new position. In retrospect, I realize that I might have interpreted it as a reason to stay put, but my interpretation in that moment was that it supported leaving. My subconscious mind may have seen the second band of rainbow as a message to step into this second administrative position. I made my decision to move forward, though I had no idea what lay ahead. I had had many experiences in both the academy and nonprofit worlds by that time, and thought I was prepared for a new challenge. A challenge it was.

The first few days on the job, three of the office staff announced their intention to quit and find other positions. I understood that this had nothing to do with me, and everything to do with what they had experienced in the recent past. The department had been in turmoil: a college dean had placed the unit in receivership before leaving the institution, which means that control over its affairs was placed in the hands of outsiders. There had been three chairpersons in two years, and to be fair, efforts had been made by these individuals to stabilize departmental conditions with new personnel policies and bylaws that defined how the department should function. A viability study had been conducted about the need for a new building. But I found a budget in the red and abdication of responsibility by the faculty. No one wanted to serve on key departmental committees or in the leadership positions that are so crucial to shared governance. We occupied an old converted engineering building with a legacy of health and safety violations. It was abysmal and filthy. Many individuals remained stuck in long-standing conflicts with their colleagues, which also played out among graduate and undergraduate students.

Within a month, I had hired fresh staff with whom I was eager to work. I had also begun sorting out the budget with a tough new office manager. And I had established a "common room" in the office suite that could be used by individuals or groups who wished to meet in a neutral place. I engaged our weary building proctor, working with him and a few paid students to clean up the studios, classrooms, halls, and storage areas. My faculty colleagues could hardly believe that I would lend a hand in these activities, and none of them were willing to join our crew. But we made rapid headway in creating what felt like a new, or at least renewed, facility. We requested fresh paint from the university facilities staff for the first time in decades.

Then I wrote a set of ground rules for our community interaction, which I discussed with the staff and faculty at length before they were approved, circulated, and posted prominently around the building.

Ground Rules for Interaction, Collegiality, and Communication

We work in a universe (university!) of conflicted discourse. We cannot avoid, nor should we always try to avoid, conflict. But we do need rules to guide us. Our behavior (speech and action) often mirrors or models our research and creative work, which are based in a strong individualistic ethos. Therefore, what we need is a set of shared ground rules for interaction, collegiality, and communication.

1. Respect your colleagues, both faculty and staff.
   - Treat one another as equals.
   - Practice the Golden Rule, i.e., treat others as you wish to be treated.
   - Practice compassion, forgiveness, and civility.
   - Listen with an open mind.
2. Trust that what you hear is the (other's) truth. Seek common ground.
3. Plan ahead when you have jobs that impact the staff's duties.
4. Everyone has a voice and will have time to speak.
5. Take time to communicate what people ought to know.
6. Collegiality means civility and shared responsibility.

Those early weeks involved long twelve- and fourteen-hour workdays, seven days a week. It took me a year to winnow this down to a six-day-a-week job, and another year to move to a five-day work schedule. I certainly experienced a range of emotions, from excitement to frustration and anger. Lacking the wisdom that develops through self-reflection, we may act out unconscious values of impatience or anger related to our wish to control particular situations. I once sought to generate greater feelings of equanimity by writing the word "aversion" on the white board in my office and ticking off the number of times I felt this strong negative emotion. I diligently tried to remain clear about the values I expressed verbally and through my actions.

Even though the challenges of this position continued in subsequent years, there were also rewards, both immediate and over the long-term, which accrued from the manner in which I began my service as chair of the department. Both faculty and staff were responsive to our ground rules, and our meetings began to have a semblance of civility. Within that first month in 1998, our college dean, Peter Spear, allocated the funds needed to begin the program planning for a new facility. The planning process for a new visual arts complex was enormously uplifting for staff, faculty, and students. No matter the difficulties we face, a new place to begin in our lives can always be found.[3]

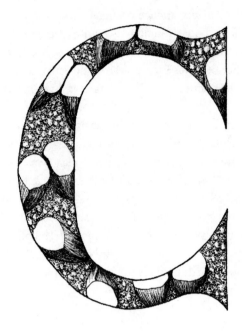

Change

Prepare yourself for change, for this is the way of the world.

ORGANIZATIONAL CHANGE IS A complex journey and process. Perhaps this truism barely warrants mention, but I do not intend the statement to be limited to sweeping strategic and operational change. I am thinking about both the effort involved in working toward major and minor institutional goals, and the commitment to your own personal change and transformation. When you become a leader in an organization, both are necessary, even inevitable. You may, to begin with, be less interested in organizational change than in maintaining the functioning status quo. But like all of nature, neither human beings nor organizations are static. Individuals come and go, groups evolve. Change is inevitable.

I have always been engaged by John Keats's idea of negative capability. In considering Shakespeare's character in a letter to his brother, Keats described this as a unique inner state: the capacity to live amidst uncertainty, mystery, or doubt without grasping for reasons; the ability to hold contrary views in one's mind and to experience contradiction or conflict without grasping after facts. This, for Keats, was negative capability: a unique skill for facing seemingly difficult or "negative" experiences with an open mind and heart.

Throughout the process of confronting change, ask yourself, "How am I doing? What is working and what should I change?" Like a professor who uses midterm student evaluations to determine the effectiveness of a course, listen to your colleagues and friends. Ask for feedback about what is happening, but be wary of the tendency to make inappropriate assumptions. Years ago, I read a trenchant theological essay by Valerie Saiving in which she said that women sin through self-abnegation, while men sin through self-assertion.[4] "Sin" is one of those strong words, loaded with cultural and religious baggage. We might simply say "err" instead. Women err when they negate the self too often, while men err when they assert the self too often. Obviously, this is a generalization, but it is worthwhile to analyze how gender, ethnicity, class, age, and ability affect your openness to and perception of change.

As Jane Hirshfield has written, "Everything changes; everything is connected; pay attention."[5] Although this is Hirshfield's seven-word definition of Buddhism, I think it is also a fine summary of how a leader should approach change. As the present heads into the unknown future, possessing the ability to face inexorable processes of change with equanimity will save your life.

Digitality

Confronting the challenges of our digital age, we should be like
the ancient Roman god Janus who had two faces, one looking back
into the past, the other looking toward the future.

IN BOOKS AND ARTICLES dating from the early 1990s, philosophers and
writers have used the word "digitality" to name the fundamentally new
condition of our lives. For instance, Jean Baudrillard used the word criti-
cally in his 1994 book, *Simulacra and Simulation*, to describe how we are
caught in constant polarities in the move from analog to digital processes.
More than a decade later, Martin Lister described digitality as a condition
in which texts are dematerialized, literally separated from their material
form. Data is compressed, then accessed at high speeds and in nonlinear
ways, where it can be easily manipulated.

On the other side of such critical and descriptive approaches is Nicholas Negroponte's optimistic vision of "being digital," as the title of his 1995 book put it. Negroponte helped to found the Massachusetts Institute of Technology's Media Lab. More recently, he took a leave from his work at MIT in order to found One Laptop Per Child, a project that seeks to put rugged, low-cost, low-power computers in the hands of children around the world.[6] Negroponte's vision of the future is clear. Technology will bring human beings everywhere, rich and poor, into closer connection with one another, and this will lead to a brighter future for all.

I am not so sanguine or confident. We are in the midst of a revolution in the technologies that mediate our experience of ourselves and the world. But this revolution is also a game of seduction and betrayal, for the immediate gains of technology are also followed by long-term liabilities. Automobiles have led to degradation of the air, developments in medicine to ever more resilient viruses, and nuclear science to increased radioactivity in the environment. Computers and mobile devices have led to compromised privacy, thanks to malware and database hacking. They also extend the impact of electromagnetic fields on our bodies, creating a lack of silence and space for solitude.

Yes, the World Wide Web, e-mail, blogs, and social media are interactive, immediate, and ubiquitous. We have the possibility of being in continuous contact with others no matter where we are, but is this really necessary? Our lives are consumed with managing these technologies, but to what end? In 1990, Donna Haraway coined the term "informatics" to describe these "scary new networks" that dominate every aspect of our social, cultural, and biological lives.[7] Certainly, I am curious about the new worlds unfolding before me in their networked glow. Simultaneously, I hear Neo-Luddites stamping and shouting, breaking things. What they say resonates with my basic apocalyptic orientation: All resources will be wrested from the earth and biosphere, all life annihilated. The world will die. Our march to Cyberia may seem full of pleasurable entertainments at the moment, but it will end in imprisonment. Neo-Luddite critics of our digital age may be this century's prophets. We would do well to heed their cries.[8]

METAPHORIC DIGRESSION: THE FUTURE OF DIGITALITY

I read E. M. Forster's short story, "The Machine Stops," during my first year of college in the late 1960s. At that time, I was naively impressed by his idea that our choices are guided by the memory of birth and the expectation of death. Years later, while conducting research about the impact of electronic media in contemporary life, I encountered references to the story, which I only vaguely remembered. Originally published in 1909 in the *Oxford and Cambridge Review*, this was Forster's only attempt to write futuristic science fiction. I found the story in Forster's 1928 collection, *The Eternal Moment.* Wandering around the lowest basement of my university library where the old Dewey decimal system books were stored, I searched until I located the proper aisle, pulled the volume from its place, and settled onto a nearby stool to read this mesmerizing narrative once again. It remains as chilling now as it was the first time I read it, so long ago.

In the story, a woman named Vashti lives alone in a small hexagonal underground room, "like the cell of a bee," as Forster explains. About five feet tall, her face is white, like a fungus grown without light. She has neither teeth nor hair. The air is fresh, though no vents are visible. Her room contains buttons and switches used to fulfill all of her needs—for food and water, music and clothing, bathing and sleep, and for communicating with friends and delivering lectures. Everyone has a copy of *The Book of the Machine*, which contains instructions on how to live and how to deal with every contingency.

Her son Kuno calls from time to time, wanting to see her, but she usually refuses, for humans no longer raise children or touch one another. All of their contact with others is mediated by The Machine, through pneumatic posts (what we know as instant messaging or e-mail) and through blue plate-like disks, cinematophotes that transmit visual images. Early in his life, Kuno had been identified as different from others and was moved to other rooms below the surface of the earth, just like Vashti's. Now he wants to see his mother and talk in person. Vashti reluctantly agrees and makes the air-ship flight, during which she tries to avoid looking at the earth below. The desire to look directly at things in the world had lingered when air-ships were first built, but now most people shrink back from the world outside its windows.

Vashti's meeting with Kuno is described in the second of three parts in the story, and it is gripping. Kuno has made a point of exploring the world that almost everyone else avoids. Outside of The Machine's steady hum, Kuno has experienced silence, has seen trees, ferns, and another person, so he knows that there is life on the surface of the earth, so far above the underground rooms that have been their respective homes since birth. Because of his successful attempts to ascend into the earthly environment, Kuno is now threatened with "homelessness," being exposed to the air without a respirator, which would kill him.

In the story's third part, Forster describes further social developments in Vashti's and Kuno's world. Respirators are abolished. In lectures on the cinematophote, everyone is urged to beware of "first-hand ideas" and told, "Let your ideas be second-hand." Religion, which had waned, is reestablished with people worshipping diverse aspects of The Machine, such as the blue optic plates through which they see one another, or the Book itself, bound and gilded for each person.

Then the final disaster begins. Curious gasping disfigures the music Vashti loves. As with other people, she adapts to jarring noises, moldy artificial fruit, stinking bath water, and defective rhymes on the poetry machine. But then the beds fail to appear when summoned, which leads to growing discontent. Finally, she learns that the "Mending Apparatus," which had kept everything functioning, is in need of repair. The light begins to fail, the air becomes foul, and it is clear that the machine is running down and will stop, as Kuno has predicted. Approaching the end, Vashti finds her son in the tunnels outside her room, which are full of bodies of the dead. He is bloody, dying in the poisoned darkness. They kiss and speak a few final words before everything explodes. "Some fool will start the Machine again, tomorrow," she says. Kuno replies that this will never happen: "Humanity has learnt its lesson."

Now that I have told you this tale, I urge you to read its prescient message for yourself. Would that *we* might learn its lessons.

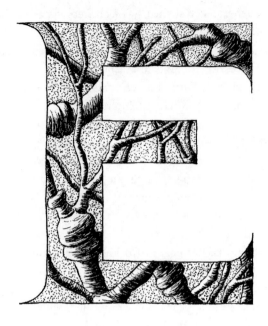

Energy

We are like dandelions. Root and shoot move in opposite directions, into the earth and toward the light. To be grounded yet alive in the world—this is energy.

THE CHINESE CONCEPT OF *Qi* or *Chi* represents the fundamental life force that courses through all sentient beings. It is the energy associated with growth. In plant geometry, the point where energy moves up toward the light and down with gravity is called the "lemniscate." The word originated with the Swiss mathematician, Jacob Bernoulli, who gave this name to a figure-eight shaped curve in 1694. Derived from the Latin word *lemniscatus*, hanging ribbon, it became associated with the infinity symbol, and the Möbius strip, a form having no inside or outside. St. Thomas Aquinas used the symbol to describe the circular movement of angels. In the twentieth century, scientists George Adams and Olive Whicher worked with theories of projective geometry and plant forms, defining the lemniscate as I am using it here. I learned of this concept from writer, potter, and poet M. C. Richards after she had studied with Whicher in England.

Think of a dandelion. The gesture of the plant—its directional movement—radiates from a midpoint. As foliage and flower, it follows the sun. As root, it grows so deep that when I try to disentangle it from the earth, I usually pull out a stub. The lemniscate is that place in a plant where the energy of explosion and growth moves up, and the force of gravity compels the dandelion to grow down. The crossing point between the root and the shoot, the lemniscate is a metaphor for qualities that characterize a fine leader, an inviolable center from which one's energy manifests both toward the self, and outward into the world.

I remain grateful to teachers in the arts especially, teachers who helped me to understand that outer processes in the world can point toward inner life. I learned about the lemniscate and crossing point from M. C. Richards, as mentioned earlier, and she offered other powerful archetypal images that affected my initial experiences in ceramics. Centering clay on the potter's wheel and centering the self in a fragmented world, the power of evolution and change, made visible in the mystical transformative fire of the kiln—these nearly always produced the unexpected. David Stannard shared his love of geology and knowledge of physics, which took me not only out into the world of rocks and water, but also toward practices of mindful attention. He encouraged me to observe a candle for a long time, long enough to understand the colors of heat and processes of convection and radiation. I also learned that watching a candle is a traditional way to learn concentration and meditation. Bob James, a committed leader in my university, egged me on in the creative life, no matter what mistakes or feeble results seemed to emerge at first. That capacity to keep going, no matter what, has evolved into steady perseverance in my adult life. George Kokis shared, through example, how to give form to mystical longing and insight, a process that continues into his old age.

What I learned from these teachers has helped me to find the leader's lemniscate: a place inside that allows me to be rooted in the earth, yet fully engaged in the human world. I know how to center myself and I am curious about and eager to learn from processes of growth and change. Early experiences of practicing mindful attention and from experiencing failure have contributed to my ability to concentrate and persevere in the face of adversity. And my ongoing commitment to the inner spiritual life . . . this has indeed become a compass on my leadership path.

Foresight

Be cognizant of the past and mindful in the present, but keep one
eye on the future. To be able to reconcile the prosaic
and visionary is a unique skill worth cultivating.

I BELIEVE THAT THE future is at risk. Over the past two decades, I have written broadly about the reclamation of the future (a seemingly contradictory
phrase) and about the importance of nurturing the capacity for apocalyptic
imagination. Foresight does not sound so grand. But if the future is uncertain, then it behooves us to nurture this sensibility. Foresight is the ability to
foresee the likely consequences of an action or situation. It is hard to define
but easy to identify when we experience it in ourselves or see it in others.
Foresight means that, having taken in the lessons of the past and realities
of the present, we try to imagine possible future consequences of our own

and others' actions. It combines intuition with astute seeing of what is and with imagination. Foresight is linked to prescience, knowledge of events before they occur. Although we might associate prescience with mystical or clairvoyant insight, it is actually possible to foster this ability through vision and imagination. Although little studied, foresight deserves our attention.

INSTRUCTIONS TO MY SON ON HIS 38TH BIRTHDAY

> To know the world—
> To know yourself as the world.
> To be always present in the moment.
> To be the one only you can be.
> To aspire toward being and knowing—
> To aspire to do good.
> To act as if the future mattered—
> To act,
> > for once,
> > for all.

This poem is about knowing, being, aspiring, and acting: all qualities related to intuition, clear vision, and imagination—in short, to foresight. In particular, to act *as if the future matters* means being willing to dedicate yourself toward trying to understand how your actions in the present will play out in the future. To act, *for once, for all* suggests the possibility of acting not based on the usual self-interest, but rather, to ask what might happen if we act on behalf of the greater good. This openness to imagining the possible consequences of actions and to acting on behalf of others will have a powerful formative role as you lead others into the unknown.

Garden

Observe the world and learn from nature.

GARDENING IS ONE OF my longest held passions. Some years ago, I planted fruit trees that have begun to bear fruit. Presently, I grow medicinal herbs, a few vegetables, and perennials. Bears, insects and squirrels, scorching heat, killer frosts, drought, and hail—I know a range of conditions that affect how things grow. Working in a garden over many years has fostered my perceptual abilities and powers of imagination. Like a farmer or gardener, every leader needs discerning eyes and ears, a sense of timing and rhythm, and a deep understanding of how necessary dormancy is to survival. Gardening is a profound metaphor for leadership.

I first began thinking about these connections when I edited Mary Caroline Richards's book, *Opening Our Moral Eye*. In a chapter titled "Art and Agriculture," Richards emphasized that observing how all things live and die is essential to nurture creativity and to develop both outer sight and inner vision. How do we enhance our powers of vision and imagination? Through careful observation of the natural world. Time, for instance, can be experienced through color, especially the changes in color associated with different times of day and year. Form, shade, and other visual elements also come into play. A farmer watches the sky and learns to read it through clouds, light, shadow, and stars. Through tending plants and observing the world, we learn meditative attention.

In Stephen Covey's book, *Living the Seven Habits*, I encountered the phrase "law of the farm." Covey uses the metaphor of farming to highlight the ongoing, focused attention required for growth. Just as a successful crop is dependent upon careful attention to preparing the soil, seeding, watering, and cultivating, so we, as leaders, must carefully prepare our internal ground and tend it as farmers if we are to grow. And we must attend to those we serve in the same way. Such essential principles and natural laws operate whether or not we agree with them.

FROM THE CHRONICLES OF EXPERIENCE

Every season in the garden brings new opportunities to reflect about how spirituality and leadership are related to growth and decay. I moved to the land on which I live, in the Rocky Mountain foothills, in the late 1990s. Almost immediately, I noticed a small patch of *urtica doica*, stinging nettles, growing in one area of the property. Given that I live in a relatively dry climate, I was surprised by these healthy plants, for they usually thrive where there is plenty of water. Living in the Pacific Northwest as a child, I had many encounters with nettles when I wandered in the woods. Usually, I would find myself with itchy welts on my legs, arms, and hands after scrambling through brambles. Packing mud on the welts, I felt relief, and my mother would replace the mud with calamine lotion when I got home. Slowly, I learned where not to tread, and I became wary of the damp, dark green undergrowth.

My adult interest in medicinal plants led in another direction, however, for I learned that nettles are a powerful spring tonic and effective antiallergy medicine. Before they flower in the spring, nettle leaves may be steamed, made into tea, or dried for later use. Today, I use them in all seasons when hay fever comes on, when I get a cold, or simply to boost my immune system. The other day, while I was drinking tea from fresh nettles, a friend stopped by and was alarmed. "Aren't they poisonous?" he asked. I offered him a sip, and he was surprised by their distinctive pleasant taste.

The lesson here? Appearance isn't everything. What appears to harm may actually heal, once you know how to use it. There are people who are like nettles, stinging and seemingly harmful. But once we learn how to engage those individuals, we may see another possibility—a way in which even the difficult ones can function creatively in a community.

Yet the garden teaches about toxicity, too. I often plant *datura stramonium*, jimson weed, beside the front steps of the house. This plant, like nettles, prefers damp climates, but I have been able to cultivate it as a garden annual. The smell is divine, and makes sitting on the steps with a cup of tea a distinct sensory pleasure. But this plant can kill. Even ingesting a small portion can lead to hallucinations, delirium, and death. Needless to say, on the leadership path we encounter heartbreaking situations and people who interact with others in poisonous ways. For instance, I tried repeatedly to intervene constructively in one staff personnel situation, but ultimately initiated procedures to fire this particularly toxic individual. Leaving the job, this person destroyed files containing information gathered over many years. From this I learned to make even more diligent inquiries prior to hiring a person who seemed pleasant and competent.

My experience growing and using *humulus lupulus*, hops, offers another metaphoric example. Hops are used to brew beer, but when I placed six plants along the railing of the porch that circles our house, I was more interested in its calmative properties. Less powerful than valerian as a sleep aid, I enjoy hops tea in the evening, when it also serves as a fine digestive tonic. The first year, the vines were extensive and beautiful, the buds and flowers an exquisite light green. But the second year, and for every subsequent year, the plant would be covered with aphids by the time the flowers began to appear. I could not get enough ladybugs to counter the insect destruction of the plant. I finally dug out the hops this year, after having them for nearly a decade. This proved to be a tremendous challenge because the roots were so deep. Sometimes we also need to let people go who have been with us a long time. While they may have been good employees at one time, they may no longer fit or their performance may have deteriorated. And those employees can be as difficult to unseat as the hops. One must work carefully and diligently to remove them. Similar principles apply to the leader herself. An organization may have been an appropriate fit for a long time, but then becomes so toxic that we must remove ourselves. Likewise, some programs, policies, and products work for a lengthy period, then are no longer effective. We must have the willingness and courage to expunge them when that happens.

This part of the garden, where the hops had been, is now resting, dormant for a season or two, as I muse about what to plant there. I am not in a hurry to fill this empty space. The capacity to wait and to observe is an essential quality on the leadership path, for often it is not clear what to say or do in a given situation. I have experienced this repeatedly, especially during eight years of building a new program from scratch. What renovations to undertake, what courses to initiate in this visual and performing arts program, which faculty to hire, how to reach out to students. These questions begged for immediate answers. But I proceeded slowly, waiting when necessary until the next steps were clear. There was a deep spiritual resonance in this waiting, too, an attitude of attention and openness to momentary insight. When I left that leadership position after eight years, I left a thriving program in good hands.

A committee, department, or organization is a living, breathing entity that grows and diminishes by turns, subject to the same laws of nature that cause a plant to reseed itself, be dormant, and then grow when water, sun, and warmth combine. As a leader, your work will involve this kind of careful and timely cultivation. I began this chapter with the suggestion that observing the world and learning from nature are important practices on the leadership path. Tending the land is a metaphor for how we care for and serve others. You may find it generative to muse about what grows in the garden you have inherited in your leadership position. Wait. Watch. Ask yourself what it should become. Then, dig.

Hope

Hope is a memory of the future.

HOPE IS DIFFICULT TO describe, even mysterious, and it is inextricably linked to despair.[9] Despair is an attitude of capitulation and acceptance, while hope implies a relaxed form of nonacceptance. Hope never fully accepts what is as the finalized end, but expresses this nonacceptance in an attitude of relaxation and patience. In hoping, we acknowledge the existence of creative powers in the universe and appeal to them to work their magic in ways that we may not comprehend. In hoping, we also express our optimism about basic human goodness.

Hope implies a special relationship to and consciousness of time. Despair sees time as a prison, closed and finalized. Hope is prophetic, not in the sense that it sees what will be, but it affirms the future *as if* it sees what will be. *Hope is a memory of the future.* What a strange and counterintuitive statement. Hope refuses to see time as closed, but understands that time is a spiraling continuity where the present connects past and future. Hope claims nothing and does not insist upon its rights to anything in particular, but it waits. How do we make sense of this central paradox? Hope implies a powerful role for memory, for it is only with a robust memory of what *was* that we may imagine a different future than the one we seem to be living ourselves into at a given juncture. Integral to the process of waiting and imagining is the willingness to take risks, to consider alternatives and to be willing to walk toward the unknown. Certainly, some of us would argue that hope implies desire for a specific end, but in my view, to hope means *not* to be caught in a mesh of immediate needing and wanting. In fact, the desire to have and to possess—objects, experiences, particular attainments—stands in the way of hope, for this sets up expectations that may not be fulfilled. Hope is a form of imaginative remembering that brings past and future into one word. Hope, like love, is a gift; it cannot be bought.

But where does hope come from, and why do we hope? These are clearly difficult questions to answer. Hope is like other virtues such as kindness, generosity, discipline, and patience. It can be refused, or cultivated. Perhaps, in the end, we hope simply because we are human, thinking and feeling sentient beings.

Throughout the chapters of this *Abecedary*, I return to themes that will serve and support you in your roles as an administrator and leader. Sometimes, due to the course of our life, our fate or destiny, we are propelled to consider the shape of our most fundamental values and worldview at an early age. Sometimes, we grow into such reflection later. One of the central premises of this book is that developing the inner life will offer both depth and breadth to your leadership style. This, at least, is my hope.

Impermanence

Knowing that change is inexorable and that all phenomena are
impermanent leads to a deep visceral awareness of the need to
reevaluate one's values and approach to life.

THE POWER OF DEVELOPING this awareness of impermanence is that it
makes us more compassionate toward ourselves and others. Because we
know that all things will pass and that all conditions will change, we can be
less reactive in situations of difficulty. This is especially relevant when a person in leadership reaches the point of wondering if, and trying to determine
when, it is time to move on. Fine leaders know when to leave positions of
leadership. Often this point comes when the challenges of the job are gone
and dissatisfactions are greater than satisfactions. Preparing for one's own
demise is therefore an important principle and tool in the leadership kit.

The main thing is not to stay in a position because others want you to or because you feel a sense of obligation or fear that no one else can do the job. There is inevitably a feeling of a small death in the process, but it is not to be feared. As revered teacher Patrul Rinpoche wrote, "Impermanence is everywhere, yet I still think things will last. I have reached the gates of old age, yet I still pretend I am young. Bless me and misguided beings like me, that we may truly understand impermanence."[10]

METAPHORIC DIGRESSION: DEATH AND DYING

My awareness of and curiosity about death came early in my life, before adolescence, when my mother attempted suicide. As a teen, I attempted to deal with the consequences of that experience by reading widely in existential and Jungian psychology, from Otto Rank and Abraham Maslow to Carl Jung and James Hillman.

Decades later, following the deaths of six people in my life within an eight-month period, I took part in a grief group organized by my local hospice center. Subsequently, I decided to undertake hospice training in order to work with the dying. My training turned into an extensive process of more than eighty hours of workshops, reading, and study about both Western and Eastern perspectives on death and dying. I became an active volunteer with hospice in 2008. While it is hard to encapsulate why I am doing this, there are at least five compelling reasons.

First, studying diverse teachings about death from Christian, Jewish, and Buddhist traditions is more than just a conceptual preparation for dying. It is a way to relate to challenges in daily life. These include difficulties with my reactions to thoughts, feelings, and events, but I find such study particularly helpful when facing difficulties in relationships with others.

This relates to the second point: that these teachings are helpful in dealing with anything that ends and the general fact that everything changes. I cannot avoid the reality of change when I am caring for a dying hospice patient.

Third, embracing impermanence and reframing life as a process of dying has quite literally transformed my perceptions and brought me to life. Who cannot find joy in the beauty of the world?

Precarious Beauty

I am the snake curled in the summer sun.
I am the creek half-covered with ice.
I am the grass with razor sharp edges.
I am the ice whose clear body hugs stone.
I am the coolness of marble.
I am the willow undulating in strong wind.
I am the chickadee flitting through aspen and plum.
I am the first dipper of spring, bowing in water.
I am the branches grounded after last night's storm.
I am the one who sees the moment that flees.

Fourth, we swim in an ocean of death. I still vividly remember a child-hood experience of burying a dead bird in the neighbor's backyard. Later, looking around at things that were dying—even seasonally, like oak leaves on the tree in front of my apartment—I found solace in the cycles of grow-ing, dying, and dormancy. Coming upon an exquisite dead swallowtail, I brought it into the studio and drew the butterfly in colorful detail.

Finally, a fifth reason that I have been drawn to work with those who are dying concerns my efforts to become a better leader. Facing the reality of death and dying has given me a renewed lightness and sense of humor in my personal and professional lives. In material terms, I still seek comfort at home and work hard to achieve ambitious goals in my work. But my inner life has deepened in multifarious and ineffable ways that help *to hold* and sustain me through the challenges of administration and leadership. The psychologist Donald Winnicott introduced the idea of a "holding environ-ment" modeled on the mother-child relationship, and he extended it into both the therapeutic relationship and the wider experience of an individual in the world.[11] Contemplative and mindfulness practices, and especially those that deal with death and dying, have become such holding environ-ments for me. Bringing these practices into my workspace—alone at my desk, in conversation, or as I walk between meetings—has given me un-expected resources for meeting the challenges of leading others effectively.

In *Living in the Light of Death* Larry Rosenberg outlined a meditation that had been described in detail by the Indian Buddhist teacher Atisha (980–1054 CE).[12] Structured as three major points, each of which has three aspects, this meditation looks at the certainty and imminence of death. It is intended to motivate us to make the best use of our lives, and continues to inform my daily meditations.

Death is inevitable. There is no possible way to escape death.

1. Everyone will die. Not even the most revered leaders have lived indefinitely. Of the current world population of over seven billion people, few will be alive in one hundred years.

2. The remainder of our life span continually decreases. Life has a definite, inflexible limit, and each moment brings us closer to the finality of that limit. We are, from this perspective, dying from the moment we are born.

3. Death will come whether or not we have made time to prepare for it. Death comes in a moment and its time is often unexpected. Given this reality, we might usefully ask ourselves how best to spend this precious time that remains.

The cause and time of death are uncertain.

4. Our life expectancy is uncertain, as the young can die before the old and the healthy before the sick.

5. There are many causes of and circumstances that lead to death. Even things that sustain life, such as food and transportation, can kill us.

6. The human body is fragile, and this contributes to life's uncertainty. The body can be easily destroyed by disease, accidents, or other disasters.

Only our mental and spiritual development can help at the time of death.

7. Worldly possessions and wealth will not help us.

8. Our relatives, friends, and loved ones can neither prevent our death, nor die with us.

9. Even our own body cannot help as we approach death. We have to leave it behind like a winter coat or an old pair of shoes.

Where does this leave those of us on the leadership path? Certainly, I do not mean these reflections to provoke pessimism or resignation. Recently, rereading *Lifework*, a small book by poet Donald Hall about his methods and practice of writing, I was taken by his idea that work can be a defiance of death. "If work is no antidote to death, nor a denial of it, death is a powerful stimulus to work. *Get done what you can.*"[13] So, knowing that all things are impermanent, keep values of compassion and discipline at the forefront of your awareness as *you* get done what you can.

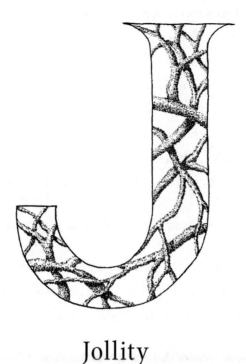

Jollity

Cultivate humor about the human condition. The only way I know to do this is to avoid seeing everything as permanent and solid.

I WAS A SERIOUS child, tending toward the sober and somber. Only in my middle age, since undertaking my leadership path, have I understood the absurdity of my weak sense of humor. This is my Achilles heel, my tragic flaw and fatal weakness. Neither Cheerios nor Wonder Bread helped. What I needed was a good dose of "Directives for the Director":

1. Jabber incoherently from time to time.

2. Jangle your spurs when your mulish mind won't move.

3. Jazz up your office with photographs of yourself in this year's Halloween costume.

4. Jerk yourself out of somnolence by singing your favorite tune.

5. Jest about your inability to jest.

6. Jingle your keys every time you walk by a mirror.

7. Jockey for a front row seat at the Comedy Palace.

8. Jog over to the cosmetics counter and buy black lipstick.

9. Join a clown troupe for a weekend.

10. Joke about yourself, not others.

11. Jolt your memory about something funny that happened earlier today.

12. Jot down jokes so you can pull them out of your pocket when needed.

13. Journey to the ends of the earth and come back to tell the tale.

14. Joust with reporters who have come by to hear what happened.

15. Judge what the truth is, then turn it upside down to see the other truth.

16. Juggle your cookies and teacup while shaking hands with your colleague as she walks in.

17. Jumble the bricks of your solid thoughts until they crumble into dust.

18. Jump for joy whenever you get a chance.

19. Junk your old habits of mind.

20. Jut not your chin or chest, but project your kind heart.

21. Juxtapose the serious with the amusing and see where joy lies.

Avoid . . . seeing . . . everything . . . as . . . permanent . . . and . . . solid.

Kitchen

What does it mean to nurture others?

THINK ABOUT THE ROLE of food and drink in the life of your department, unit, or organization. If there isn't already one, create a space with an electric water pot, a refrigerator, and a microwave, which I consider minimum requirements for any office suite. Keep this small kitchen stocked with tea, coffee, and healthy refreshments. If this isn't part of the budget, take up a collection. Or, knuckle down when necessary and purchase refreshments yourself. Demonstrate your commitment by cleaning the kitchen from time to time. Kindle appreciation for this nurturing role by cooking for your friends and colleagues or by taking them out to eat. I do not mean to imply any gender limitations here, for women and men are equally able to carry out these recommendations.

What I am suggesting is that feeding others has both literal and figurative benefits. Who has not experienced the pleasure of hearing the sighs and expressions of appreciation of friends and family at the end of a meal, whether prepared and eaten at home, at a picnic, or at a restaurant? Once, when I brought a tray of sweets from the finest bakery in Boulder to a crucial meeting about our facilities, I was encouraged by the exclamations of pleasure that my colleagues expressed. Our dialogue resulted in a series of previously unforeseen opportunities and tremendous enthusiasm. Later, holding a formal daylong retreat to plan for the upcoming academic year, I made sure that the two major meals and refreshments were of the finest quality. I had learned long before in working for nonprofit organizations that food could play either a supportive role, or it could serve as an impediment to the business at hand. These literal examples cannot really be separated from the figurative benefits that can accrue from remembering the kitchen. To nurture others in myriad ways, physically, is thoroughly connected with nurturing their development and engagement in shared goals.

TWO RECIPES

Nine Root Soup

Dice lots of garlic, onions, and ginger to taste.
(Rule of thumb: a thumb size root of ginger for one pot.)
Then,
chunk or slice
three carrots,
one or two yellow or red potatoes,
one large sweet potato,
one turnip,
one rutabaga,
two parsnips,
and put into stock or water.
Add meat or not.
Cook until done.
Augment with sour cream, chives, or cilantro.
Serve as is or puree.
Eat with gusto, with six to eight others.

Ode to James Beard and Sharon D. Welch[14]

Melt four ounces of chocolate and ½ cup of unsalted butter
    in a double boiler.
Stir in one cup sugar and one teaspoon vanilla.
Set aside to cool slightly.
Measure one cup of mixed flours (brown rice, amaranth, quinoa, millet)
    with ½ teaspoon salt.
Mix dry ingredients into melted ingredients.
Whip two or three eggs.
Hardly stirring, add eggs with nuts or seeds, if desired.
(Roasted unsalted cashews, pine nuts, and freshly ground flaxseed
    are good.)
Bake for 30 minutes at 325 degrees in a pie tin.
Cut into tiny slivers and serve.
The best non-gluten chocolate brownies!

Leadership

The root of the word leadership may be traced to the Indo-European root *leit*, to go forth, to die.

AN ENORMOUS AMOUNT HAS been written about leadership. I have found it helpful to think about what leadership means to me, what my skills and style are, and how I might supplement habitual ways of thinking with new ideas and attitudes. To lead is to offer guidance and direction, to show the way by going in advance. Leadership means moderation and finding the middle way between indulgence and asceticism. But let me attend to the hardest part first. Giving so much of one's energy, talent, and creativity to the workplace also entails sacrifice. The time and energy one puts into creating community—building and carrying forward a collective vision, communicating to various constituencies that define the organization, and so forth—is time not spent doing other activities. Spending time with family and friends and finding time for creative solitude may be sacrificed for a while. "For a while" is the key phrase. I believe that it is useful to think of service, like the seasons, as a cyclical process, punctuated by periods of professional renewal and personal focus.

Although becoming a leader has great potential rewards, very seldom have I heard anyone acknowledge that this process also involves personal sacrifice. Perhaps leaders rarely speak about this because sacrifice is an old-fashioned word, overlaid with unwelcome religious overtones. Or, perhaps in our self-aggrandizing culture where immediate gratification is the norm, few people would be drawn to an activity if it called for self-sacrifice or self-denial. But leadership is a calling to serve within the community, to use one's skills, aptitudes, and vision for the greater good and to sacrifice other more personal goals, if only for a discrete period of time. The main question is: How can you give form to what you care the most about? Is it possible that chairing a department or running a company might be an effective mode for your work in the world? What is the role of sacrifice, and when is it time to stop sacrificing for the greater good? As you contemplate the role of sacrifice, remember that there is no knowledge without sacrifice. To state the obvious, I would not have gained both pragmatic and more intangible insights about leadership without my willingness to sacrifice personal goals in order to focus *for a while* on the greater good.

As part of your professional renewal, find mentors with whom you can speak honestly about your values and aspirations. Every good leader will inevitably encounter the dilemma of whether they should lead where they are—that is, remain in their current position—or move up. One wise dean once told me that he had put his own research into the drawer. Another redefined his scholarship through publishing personal narratives, which were a new genre for him. Still another depended upon his lab and a cadre of collaborators to further his research. Many strategies can be effective. Each of us must practice careful discernment in order to make choices about which path to take, for each direction involves its own choices and forms of sacrifice.

METAPHORIC DIGRESSION: PATH

The original metaphor for path comes from the experience of making journeys on foot or horseback when the known world was a network of trails. Paths were everywhere; they were clearly visible, worn by the action of many feet, sometimes marked by stones or posts to measure or indicate distance. The word path is a noun, a place for movement. Yet it also implies action, for on a path we are usually going somewhere: we process. By analogy, the leadership path may be conceptualized both as a place or stage in personal development, and as a series of actions that one takes. The path worn into deep ruts by others may not be the path suitable for you as a leader who finds him- or herself on the journey. Often, finding one's way is a matter of getting off that well-worn path to move in new directions across unfamiliar terrain.

The word itself is derived from Old English *pæth*, and from the Indo-European root, *pent*, which means to tread or go. The most common dictionary definitions include a trodden track or way; a road, way, or track made for a particular purpose; the route or course along which something travels or moves; and a course of action or conduct. Repetition and reiteration are expected. To paraphrase John Dixon Hunt, a designated path or particular route may be undertaken not merely to get somewhere or perform a task, but with a higher objective.[15] Segments or fragments of the path may evoke special images, though the whole is what lends meaning and legitimacy.

In Asian cultures there are many words for path. The Chinese *Tao* is a complex word. It means way, road, or trail, but it also means to lead or follow, as well as the nature and way of truth. The Japanese *do* has various meanings, including *kado*, the way of flowers, *bushido*, the way of the warrior, and *sado*, tea ceremony. The Zen master Dogen said that "practice *is* the path."[16] In traditional Tibet, the *kora* was a pilgrim path, used for circumambulation as a way of gaining merit and paying homage to those who reside or had resided in a place. Traditionally, Tibetans believed that connection to the land is the most important way of maintaining the human life force, and that the world is now divided between those who live close to the land and those whose lives are severed from it. Traveling a *kora* was one way to maintain that connection to place. I find the idea of the *kora* particularly evocative. The idea of walking in circles may be reminiscent of thinking in circles, where there seems to be no clarity and no end to confusion. But, the *kora* is a meditative path that puts one in direct contact with the earth. Rather than using an indoor track to run, jog, or walk, why not create your own outdoor circumambulation path that helps you connect directly to place and space, to where you are, in this moment?

These definitions of path are suggestive in relation to leadership. Yes, repetition and reiteration are expected, but you must keep higher objectives in view. Ultimately, this meeting, this day, or even this year cannot encapsulate the long-term objectives of your work as a leader. For this, you need a vision of the long horizon, a sense that space extends in all directions, not just on a narrow path in front of you. Coming out of the canyon in the Rocky Mountain foothills where I live, this insight becomes tangible for me. Instead of viewing only a fragment of sky, suddenly a vista stretches toward the eastern prairies, as far as I can see. The roads lead in defined directions, but the path ahead is nonetheless spacious.

There are certainly many ways to move along the leadership path, which may be related to the ways in which we proceed down any path. You may walk in the spirit of ritual procession or meditation; stroll, ramble, or move at random; tarry or saunter; or feel compelled to linger. The stroll, exemplified in Chinese garden and path designs, is midway between procession and ramble. It implies a purpose and destination, deliberateness, a defined route, and the idea of a view of what is ahead. Facing major decisions, you may find it beneficial to step outside for a stroll. The ramble has no particular external prompt, and is directed by curiosity. It may be the most apt metaphor for walking when we have no idea what is needed most. But I find this kind of random movement more fitting when I have just completed a task or project. What could be better than meandering outside at such a moment with openness toward what is around? On paths, the width determines how many people may walk together. Steepness or grade determines speed, as does the surface, whether of earth, gravel, or smooth stone. More than once I have found it helpful to invite a colleague or coworker to join me on a challenging uphill climb in the nearby Flatirons in order to discuss thorny problems, or to mosey along the Boulder Creek path as we muse about possible future directions. Alone, I sometimes stride briskly on my leadership path; sometimes I amble, watching the play of light and shadow. Sometimes, when I need to think deeply, I walk as a form of mindfulness meditation, placing each foot slowly and deliberately in front of the other, eyes downcast.

TEN RECOMMENDED ACTIVITIES ON THE LEADERSHIP PATH[17]

1. Activate awareness, in general, and self-awareness, in particular.

2. Heal yourself and foster others' healing, knowing that most of us want wholeness.

3. Listen actively.

4. Empathize with others, while remaining grounded in your own experience.

5. Practice persuasion and consensus building in making decisions, rather than exercising coercion.

6. Develop imagination and extend your vision.

7. Foster foresight.

8. Steward resources for the greater good.

9. Commit to helping others grow.

10. Build community around issues that are specific to the needs of the group.

Mindfulness

Research in neuroscience demonstrates that mindfulness
practice—moment-by-moment present awareness—has
powerful effects on feelings of well-being, combating depression,
and enhancing memory.

MINDFULNESS IS THE PRACTICE of opening ourselves to both outer and
inner worlds simultaneously. As I type these words, tea cools in the cup
besides me. It is dark outside. Squinting through the window, I see that
snow covers the ground. I sip Japanese sencha, my favorite green tea, which
is earthy yet sweet. The rim of my handmade teacup feels uneven as I wrap
my lips around it. What is happening to Japanese tea production since
Fukushima? What about the farmers, the land itself? The heater makes a
soft hissing sound, like tinnitus. An edgy anxiety. My gut aches, a familiar

tightness that I associate with gluten, eggs, too many nuts. Ruth's cremation is later this morning, and I must buy flowers on the way to the mortuary. No one else is up yet and the house is quiet. My mind chatters, my body insists. And on and on.

Mindfulness *practice* implies more than such mindful awareness. To practice not only suggests discipline, repetition, and habit, but also listening, thinking, and examining one's experience through self-reflection and introspection. Practice means paying attention to one's thoughts, bodily sensations, speech, and action, moment by moment. Through meditating we may familiarize ourselves with a new way of being in the world. What exactly is going on in the present moment? This is a good question to ask yourself, frequently.

Mindful contemplation can be described as a way of knowing, an epistemology that is distinct from rationalist-empiricist thought. Psychologist Tobin Hart has written that an epistemology of contemplation is based on our natural ability to know through silence, by looking inward, pondering deeply, and witnessing the contents of our consciousness. In a world beset by conflict, to cultivate only critical thinking and analysis leads to partial knowing. Mindfulness is a common human activity that, when brought consciously into business and institutional contexts, offers us a new relationship with ourselves, others, and the world. It proposes an epistemology based not on data, information, and the separation of subject and object, but on knowledge, wisdom, and insight about the interconnectedness of all things. Such mindful inquiry can lead to individual transformation.

Though I presently work in a secular university context, I believe that values of respect, participation, and interconnectedness are relevant to all organizational settings, as well as to our lives more generally. Mindful inquiry is, itself, respectful. Through mindfulness practices such as meditation and prayer, we learn to recognize the individuality of others. Curiously, at the same time, we learn to resist the distancing that characterizes so much of our lives. Knowing that all phenomena are interconnected, that relationships are mutually dependent, underscores such awareness. This inquiry is participatory: The world invites us to come closer to objects and to one another. It invites us to examine itself, in all of its physicality, in detail. Like the best education in any context, it is not about losing one's own consciousness and identity, but about entering into the experience of the other, insofar as this is possible. A mindful epistemology is based on developing an ability to live with uncertainty and to sustain contradictory views. Ah!

ॐ

FIVE MINDFULNESS PRACTICES

Six Points of Posture

1. First, establish a stable *seat*. Sit at the edge of a chair.

2. Second, the *legs* should be neither crossed nor stretched out. The feet are directly under the knees.

3. Third, the *hands* are placed palms down on the thighs.

4. Fourth, the *torso* is relaxed. The spine should be straight, tilting neither to the front nor back, left nor right.

5. Fifth, the *eyes* are kept open, gazing down at a spot about three to four feet in front of you.

6. Finally, the *mouth* should be slightly open, tongue resting against the upper palette.

Mindful Breathing

Mindful breathing helps to relax and focus the mind. Even five minutes a day can make you feel more refreshed and energetic. None of us can prevent stressful situations in life, but we can begin to learn how to control our reactions to these situations. Practicing mindful breathing can help.

Begin by adopting the six points of posture. Then bring attention to the breathing. Observe the sensations of the breath in the abdomen, diaphragm, or lungs. Or focus on the light touch of air as it enters the nostrils. Try counting the breath: on the exhalation, one; next exhalation, two; and all the way to twenty-one. Then start again at one. Depending upon your state of mind, your attention may wander in either mild or wild ways. As you observe the mind, name what it wanders to and come back to the breathing and counting. Some teachers advise saying "thinking" to oneself before returning attention to the breath. While the mind often seems impossible to tame, at times we are able to rest in a quiet and calm state that is refreshing. Once you have practiced focusing on the breathing, experiment by using bodily sensations or sounds, or by watching thoughts as the point of concentration.

Walking

In this meditation, you are mindful of your surroundings while simultaneously focusing on the movement of your body. You can do this either indoors or outdoors. If you are walking alone outdoors, do not engage in conversation with those you may encounter on your walk. Stand briefly to balance yourself and to release tension, allowing your arms to hang freely. Then begin walking at a slow but normal pace. In the beginning, place awareness on one part of each foot—big toe, space beneath foot and ground, or heel. Later, try to take note of each step—the lift of the leg, the heel making contact, the roll onto the ball of the foot, other parts of the body, breathing, body temperature, wind on the face, and so on.

This practice offers many benefits. It helps to quiet and focus the mind while providing an opportunity for personal insights to arise. It develops balance and concentration and increases stamina for meditation and mindfulness of movement more generally. Walking meditation also contributes to a general sense of well-being by relaxing the body, reviving tired muscles, stimulating circulation, assisting digestion, and minimizing sluggishness. Mindfulness of the body is more important than theorizing about our physicality.

Eye Exercises[18]

1. With *closed eyes* focus on resting and refreshing your eyes by relaxing the muscles around them. Consider what internal seeing might mean.

2. With *peripheral seeing*, soften your focus and try to see from the corner of the eyes. Sometimes it is possible to see almost 180 degrees by looking straight ahead with a soft gaze. This is an exciting expansion of vision. In our time, with the presence of screens on televisions, computers, and handheld devices, many of us have never truly experienced our peripheral vision because these screens rely on a more central focus.

3. *Looking with infant eyes* suggests seeing before naming what you see. Is it possible to look at the world as if you have never seen it before?

4. *Looking between things* offers a direct experience of both positive and negative space. The world is full of objects that define space. The area

between these objects is known as negative space. We often fail to notice the unique shapes and forms of this space.

5. Through *direct looking*, you can learn to investigate, study, and absorb the images and symbols in your environment.

Hearing and Deep Listening

Sense perceptions and impressions are a form of wealth for each of us. Ours is an ocularcentric age, focused on vision and the visual. We are therefore experienced at using the eyes. In this exercise, experiment with letting the ear be the main organ of perception, even as you look at the world. From the Greeks to contemporary mystics, the ear has been as important as the eye. One way to introduce yourself to deep listening is through music. Habituated to hyperstimulation, many of us listen to music all the time, but learning to listen effectively and *to hear* has tremendous implications for our lives. Or, simply go outside and listen to the symphony of the world.

NATURE AS AN AID TO MEDITATION

Clouds gather and disperse—
I cross my legs.
Below, pink and gray granite lie covered with ochre lichen.
Above, pine branches stretch out like a web.
Nearby, a pair of mallards lifts off from the pond.
Ants,
    tingling in my right calf.
Ripple of aspen trees, not yet turning—
    pine and gentian, an unlikely pair.
Sounds of a flute drift across marsh and meadow,
    mingle with wind and gunshot.
A hummingbird startles, whizzes by too close.

Net

All things are connected.

For most of us, the obvious association with "net" is network, as in the screens that pervade our lives and connect us to the rest of the world, as well as the network of family, friends, and colleagues who sustain us. But here I am thinking of Indra's Net, an image from Hindu mythology. Indra was one of two ancient Vedic gods. In his cosmic aspect, he was seen as the liberator of the waters; in his earthly aspect, he embodied virtues of courage and leadership as the Aryan war god. In Vedic cosmology and mythology, his net hangs over his palace on Mount Meru, the center of the universe. In the *Agni Purana II*, 870, the net figures in an act of magic when Indra conjures armies in order to inspire terror in the enemy. Indra's Net is described as having a jewel at each vertex that reflects the other jewels. Like dew drops on a spider web, each knot in the net reflects all of the others in a totally interdependent and simultaneous way. In this way, Indra's Net is a symbol for the interconnectedness of all phenomena in the universe.

Interdependence characterizes everything. The desk at which I sit and write came from my friend Antonette after she died. Used as a studio table for years, it is full of scratches and gouges, rich in patina. Antonette bought it at a yard sale from an old woman who was disposing of her many possessions, which included five tables. A mark on the table leg indicates its manufacture at a furniture factory in the Pacific Northwest, where it was made from a tree that grew in conifer forests now harvested on a regular basis. There, seedlings grow from nurse logs, the decaying remains of fallen trees. Nourished by sun and precipitation, including acid rain and particles from distant volcanic eruptions, the tree that became this table is connected to the air, wind, earth, water, and space itself.

In reflecting about human existence, Italo Calvino noted that "Each life is an encyclopedia, a library, an inventory of objects, a series of styles, and everything can be constantly shuffled and reordered in every way conceivable."[19] One might add that every life, even the tree that became my table, is the result of thoroughly interrelated causes and conditions that have been shuffled and reordered throughout time. This is a profound principle that should direct and influence our work.

We grow in our ability to lead others through deep understanding that each person holds their own contradictions and confusions in tension with their capacity for clarity—all of which are the result of a life lived in distinctive ways simultaneously related with my own. The spiritual insight here is made visual and vivid in Indra's Net, which provides an image of this interconnection. I understand my colleague's suffering because I, too, have suffered. I understand his paranoia because I, too, have been afraid. I understand her joy because I, too, have felt ecstatically happy. Leadership requires, more than anything else, willingness to engage in discernment and clear seeing. Keeping Indra's Net in view enhances this aptitude.

Ontology

What makes us who we are? What is real, anyway?

ONTOLOGY BEGS US TO look closely at the nature of being, to look outside at the world around us, and to look inside at who we really are. In short, it asks us to consider *what is*. In relation to the world, what is real? What is the relationship of nature to virtual realities on our screens? In relation to the human being, what is the self and what is it becoming in this era of bionics and virtual realities? How are new technologies reshaping individual and communal identity?

A major issue, pervasive in the literature about technology, concerns what happens to actual phenomenological reality—what some of us still call "nature"—when greater value, resources, and emphasis are placed on virtual life in virtual worlds. Does the depletion of resources, pollution of the environment, breakdown of urban centers, and extinction of species *really matter* if we are anticipating a future in air-conditioned rooms, where most of our interactions are conducted through a screen, as in Forster's story "The Machine Stops"? Obviously, this is partly a rhetorical question. Nevertheless, what we value as "the real" has tremendous implications for the quality and sustainability of life.

And the self? Digital media support a model of the self that does not just play roles or have different personae, but is itself decentered, existing in various worlds and playing different roles simultaneously. These media play with our desires for self-regeneration and self-replacement, which are part of the basic quest for human identity. The danger is that they may satisfy our urge toward connection without requiring the hard work of direct confrontation and action with, or on behalf of, others.

To be on the leadership path is to be concerned with such ontological questions. Who do you want to become and what world do you want to help create?

FROM THE CHRONICLES OF EXPERIENCE

Ontological questions are not based only on the inner-outer dichotomy that I have been describing. They are also multidimensional, like a tetrahedron. A tetrahedron has four faces, each of which has three edges that form a triangle. As a whole, the tetrahedron has six edges and four vertices at each corner where three of the edges meet. It looks like a triangle-shaped pyramid, like the Pyramid of the Moon at Teotihuacan near Mexico City. I once walked alone up the steep stone steps at Teotihuacan on a windy December morning. The sky was clear when I reached the top. Extending my gaze toward the east, the south, then west and north, I felt ancient, as though I were standing at the center of the known universe in another time.

I am not a mathematician, but I find it fascinating that two tetrahedra can be put together to form a cube, and that five intersecting tetrahedra become a dodecahedron, a form known for hundreds of years. The Japanese art of origami or paper folding makes use of these mathematical insights to create everything from cranes to roses. One year, working alongside friends in a local peace and justice group, I made and strung one thousand cranes to commemorate suffering caused by the bombings of Hiroshima and Nagasaki in 1945. At the end of many hours of concentrated folding, we hung those strings of cranes on posts around the downtown municipal building. It seemed to me that I, too, was one of the poles, like a mythical *axis mundi* that connects the earth with the heavens above and underworld below. Connected to a history I did not participate in directly, I aspire to be part of a new present as it whirls into the future.

Place

Place is an ontological category, for we know *who*
we are by knowing *where* we are.

ONE'S KNOWLEDGE OF PLACE begins with bodily experience.[20] My body is
the agent and vehicle of being-in-place; it simultaneously articulates and
bears witness to that experience. This is both a descriptive and phenomenological process that may be explained in multiple ways: psychically,
architecturally, and institutionally. To make matters even more complex,
to be a body is always to be a gendered body, with a sexual orientation and
a sexual history. The body is kinetic. It moves. Yet it is also kinesthetic. It
moves and *feels*. Still, there is an ambiguous, amorphous quality to the body
in space and time. The ontological priority that must be accorded to place
extends to its relationship to the mind and body.

One of the most mundane yet significant places that affect the life of a leader is the office. I make every effort to make my office a welcoming place, and I encourage staff with whom I work to do so, too. I make a point of talking with each member of the staff every day, and I trust their individual ideas about what makes everything work. Helping with the daily functioning of the larger office suite, including keeping the office clean, aids in breaking down hierarchical barriers. Exhibiting employee or student art on the walls and keeping a bulletin board for individual achievements are effective ways of making people feel welcome.

I urge you to occupy your office every day when you are in town. Be available. Offer to help make things work, however you can. Orchestrate leadership opportunities for your colleagues. Organize the overall office for maximal functioning. Outline what needs to be done and be an active participant in these processes.

FROM THE CHRONICLES OF EXPERIENCE

When I accepted the leadership position described earlier in the *Abecedary*, I had a grandiose vision of helping to build an arts facility for the twenty-first century, *a place for art*. In itself, a grand vision can carry greatness of intent and, therefore, can spur one on. My vision served in this way.

Prior to my arrival in August 1998, the department had conducted an internal study of space needs, which was followed by a formal university feasibility study. These studies identified serious functional and life-safety deficiencies in the existing building. To clarify the issues, I immediately put together a detailed summary of previous improvements that had been made to our building, originally built in the early twentieth century. The main intractable problems concerned ventilation, drainage, inadequacy of electrical access, cooling, removal of toxic materials, and fire code violations. In fact, defining these health, life-safety, and code issues turned out to be crucial in what turned out to be more than a decade of planning and advocacy for new facilities.

With an allocation of money from the College of Arts and Sciences, we initiated a program planning process. First, we screened potential architectural firms. This was enormously exciting because they shared their ideas for what this new building might be. Once the architects for the program plan were selected, we held a series of meetings with group and individual stakeholders, including students, faculty, staff, donors, alumni, several university units, and cognate departments such as film studies and journalism. Forums were held and written questionnaires circulated.

I led and facilitated a series of daylong workshops to synthesize information gleaned from our research, to analyze our space needs, and to develop a mission statement. We needed to relate this new facility to the major institutional goals of the university and to the external constituencies within our local community, state, and region. Gathering and analyzing data about facilities alternatives, campus space, room utilization, student demographics, user groups, occupancies, and plans for what would be done with the present building all led us to a clear understanding of where we were headed.

Writing the mission statement was a constructive and joyful process, for we had the opportunity to name and articulate our vision. The new Visual Arts Complex, or VAC as we began to call it, would be a crossroads for creative activity and visual communication at the University of Colorado, Boulder, and the new home for the Department of Art and Art History and the CU Art Museum.

Following a consideration of alternatives and site requirements, we decided to recommend constructing the new Visual Arts Complex where the old building had been, although the new facility would be considerably larger. Located on the southern edge of the campus, it would become the major cultural gateway for the community. Initially, we hoped to fund the VAC through state funds and private donations. The program plan outlined that the project would cost about $45 million. The financial analysis, which included both costs and a finance plan, was completely new to me. The program plan for the Visual Arts Complex was completed on June 30, 2001, and we were eager to proceed.

Following the events of September 2001—the 9/11 disaster that changed life in so many ways—all capital projects in our state were put on hold. The program plan had taken three years to complete; I put it on the shelf. It is an understatement to say that I was disappointed. I began to understand, tangibly, that the future is never what we expect and that grandiose visions must be modified to accommodate what actually transpires. Having to leave my ego and my goals behind was a profound training in humility. I had intended to continue for subsequent terms as department chair in order to see the new building to fruition, but I decided instead to step down from my leadership position at the end of the academic year. I was satisfied that I had done as much as possible to bring my department together, and our joint work on planning the new arts center was a successful experience for all involved, even though we were unable to continue immediately. Subsequently, when I spoke with the College Dean, Todd Gleeson, about this decision, he asked if I might be willing to undertake the planning and development of a new undergraduate residential program in the visual and performing arts, part of which involved design and remodeling of the facilities. I found that prospect exciting, and began this leadership position a few months later, working on it for the following eight years.

Midway through the period of my work on the residential arts program, the original Visual Arts Complex program plan was revised and the building constructed. Garrison Roots (1952–2011), a colleague whom I greatly respected, was then chair of the department. I offered to assist him in any way I could, given my other responsibilities. I reentered the fundraising effort, helping to raise significant funds to name an art studio after artist and teacher Antonette Rosato, who had died of breast cancer a few years earlier. Later, I decided to make another gift with my husband to name an office used by visiting artists each year. Given the ambition of my original vision, this seemed a modest offering of time, energy, and money.

In the end, the state offered little financial support, and we turned to the university student government, which allocated millions of dollars over ten years through assessment of student fees. Combining these resources with ongoing donor cultivation and private fundraising, the building became a reality. The department and art museum moved in with great fanfare and celebration.

Yes, I experienced keen disappointment, but I also learned humility and modesty on my leadership path. Now, entering through dramatic tall columns into light and open space in the building foyer, I know myself in new ways.

Quarrels

"Quarrels" stand in here for all kinds and levels of conflict.
Conflicts are inevitable, but how you address them
is a matter of your attitudes and skills.

A PERSON IN A leadership position must have a fairly high tolerance for
conflict, while simultaneously being willing to name unacceptable behavior
when it occurs. A pithy summary of what I have learned through my experience goes like this: Get training and use all available resources to help
you deal with the spectrum of behavior that runs from mild quarrels and
disrespect on one end of the continuum to bullying, abuse, and physical
violence on the other end, with incivility in the center. Sadly, such behav-
iors are especially common in institutions where people have job security.

Training and resources will help, but the leader must be impeccable about assessing how her background, experiences, prejudices, hot buttons, leadership style, and temperament impact conflict—not to mention her underlying comfort level with the very concept of conflict. Then he must be equally impeccable at managing his weaknesses and capitalizing on his strengths. So, begin by assessing how you think of and handle conflict. With these few words, I identify a process that may take years. Conflict characterizes human interaction. Even a cursory understanding of history and modest attention to current events around the world underscores this point. Do not be afraid of conflict. To the extent that you can learn new ways of thinking about it, and new strategies for action, you will become an effective leader.

FROM THE CHRONICLES OF EXPERIENCE

Earlier, I noted that my work has involved responding to the unexpected. This has included addressing many conflicts. I handled issues of hate speech when offensive signs were posted on the door of our building, helping to define more clearly the university's position on free speech. I responded to a federal complaint launched by an angry faculty member and partici-pated in sexual harassment investigations initiated by students and faculty. I fired one belligerent staff assistant for refusing to do her job and initiated the process that would have resulted in firing another if that person had not moved to another position. I called the police when an angry and ag-gressive student followed me from a classroom to my office and refused to leave. Working diligently with legal counsel over several years on such issues, I also sought help from professional ombuds and mediators.

Listing such examples does little to convey the years of seemingly endless meetings, conferences, one-on-one conversations, and sleepless nights. In the process, I learned new strategies for dealing with difficult individuals, longstanding conflicts, and abdication of responsibility among colleagues. My learning came from the trenches, as well as through training in conflict resolution and mediation.

In particular, I thought I knew how to listen, but I learned more than I could have imagined about effective listening and negotiation. In training at CDR, Collaborative Decision Resources, a nationally recognized conflict

resolution center, the concept of "interests" was perhaps the most important insight for me.[21] In all negotiations, naming the procedural, psycho-
logical, and substantive interests that undergird a conflict helps to change
the problem-solving dynamic. When each of us seeks to understand the
other person's interests—what drives him, what needs she seeks to meet—
then the search can begin for alternatives that might satisfy both. This is a
complex process with many steps, but such negotiation can be enormously
creative and rewarding.

Years later, during my hospice training, we spent crucial sessions on
the key skills of deep listening.[22] Obviously, engaging with those who are
dying and with their loved ones differs from dealing with colleagues in conflict. But even there, an individual may experience various kinds of small
death. Developing the skills of a good listener involves at least three fundamental qualities, as psychologist Carl Rogers so passionately described.[23]
Empathy means entering the perceptual world of the other person and
checking to see if what I understand is accurate. Genuineness means that
I am not trying to manipulate the other or the situation. And expressing
non-possessive warmth, being present and not grasping onto my own or
the other's ideas, allows the other person to feel heard.

Deep listening is a process involving awareness, compassion, and embodied listening. Awareness is a verb here, an action: being present with
ourselves and with the other in the particular environment where we meet.
It means not being distracted—recognizing the arising of thoughts, but allowing them to leave. Like awareness, compassion is also active. We tune
in to other's state of mind—that person's anger, pain, or suffering—in order
to create a sense of connection. Being aware that I, too, experience anger
and pain becomes a ground for compassion. But how I maintain my own
boundaries in such a dialogue is crucial. While acknowledging that we exist
in interdependent relationships with others, allowing another's experience
to be their own is central to the listening process. If my negative feelings
are triggered, this shows my own ego at work, which cannot help the other.

Embodied listening means that I listen with my body, speech, and
mind. This process was well described by Eugene Gendlin in *Focusing*. To
cultivate a "felt sense" in the body helps to make conscious what we are
experiencing and to anchor us in our bodies. Such effort to develop self-
awareness is applicable in the moment of listening, for many cues and clues
can be discovered there. To the degree that I can listen to myself, I can listen
to another. Embodied listening also means that I do not rehearse what I

want to say while the other is speaking. Jumping ahead and imagining or articulating potential solutions to a problem may be counterproductive. At the least, it is a form of not listening.

How many times I have experienced precisely this process. An agitated woman strides into my office, raising her voice until she is clearly yelling about what just happened in the hallway. I think, here we go again, the same old complaint, the same anger that plays itself out again and again. I feel impatient, wishing she would leave so I could get on with the more important business at hand. When she finally exits, calmer, I close the door. Then, a loud insistent knock. A man stands in the doorway, seeking to intimidate me with demands and implied threats if I do not address his recent email, right now. I feel immediately bullied and defensive, though I do not fear the dire consequences he threatens.

Both of these responses to moments of aggression and conflict are totally understandable and legitimate. But if I am not distracted by my irritation and aversion, I might ask myself what interests are being expressed by each of these individuals. Staying conscious of my own felt experience and my bodily reactions might offer new possibilities for giving feedback to the other person. And how might I minimize the stimulation of my own negative emotions, acting like a martial artist who knows how to get out of the way when attacked? The leader who practices observing, listening, and speaking using the skills I have described here will be able to consider other possibilities, on the spot.

While working on this particular entry in the *Abecedary*, I have been carrying stones, recreating boundaries that demarcate an outdoor sanctuary. When I first moved to these foothills of the Rocky Mountains, I sat repeatedly amidst a grove of nine willows that grow about ten feet above the James Creek. One day, I moved large logs and fallen branches to demarcate the edges of the sanctuary. Eventually, with the help of neighbors, we removed the logs and put large rocks along the boundary. The northern side, which extends down a steep slope to the creek, is protected with a fence-like structure between two trees. A skilled stonemason created a patchwork floor of irregular sandstone slabs. Within the sanctuary I placed a low marble seat and marble slab, both of which I inscribed with prayers used for meditation in all seasons.

Without consulting me, my husband decided to use the boundary stones for other purposes and moved them one day. This was a source of mild, ongoing conflict between us for several years because he liked the area without its boundary markers, while I felt that he had destroyed the integrity of the sanctuary. Recently, when I insisted that it was time to repair the damage he had done, he finally acquiesced. My efforts to cajole and persuade him were eventually more effective than my anger and accusations. Sharing a life and place are like that: ongoing dialogue about differences is required.

Yesterday, I helped to move two huge pieces of granite from my medicinal garden with a backhoe. Each stone weighed over a ton. Then, one by one, I moved 104 sandstone pavers, each a mere fifteen to thirty pounds, to form part of a wall that gives me privacy when I sit in the sanctuary. Today I am filling in the interstices between other large, nondescript rocks that form the western edge. Interspersed between granite, sandstone, and gray metamorphic rocks are fist-sized fragments of white Colorado yule marble, green Connemara marble from County Galway in Ireland, slabs of light beige Vermont limestone, and black basalt from western Oregon. So much of this activity is a metaphor for the work of dealing with diverse individuals in challenging situations that call for both hard labor and crucial conversations.

I am reminded of my last departmental meeting, when six years of service as a department chair ended. I decided to give each of my colleagues a gift. I ransacked my collection of stones, gathered during travels around the world over several decades, to find appropriate offerings for each individual. I presented hefty old pestles to two individuals who had been particularly difficult. To others whose presence had been calming, I offered small red coral cabochons. Multicolored fluorite symbolized one person's ability to neutralize negativity. I gave variegated agate found on the shores of the Pacific to individuals who needed strength, or whose strength had helped others. Clear quartz crystals emphasized clarity of mind, while amethyst seemed perfect for one woman who seemed to have a healing touch. These are but a few examples of ways in which each stone served as a metaphor for what I had experienced with that person.

Spirituality and Growth on the Leadership Path

THE Q CURRICULUM, OR, HOW TO MAINTAIN EQUANIMITY
IN DIFFICULT TIMES

1. Quadruple your efforts to learn the skills of deep listening.
2. Quaff from the spring of wisdom.
3. Quail not.
4. Quake in your shoes? No, quake before a brilliant sunrise as you face a new day.
5. Qualify for your position by proving your mettle under duress.
6. Quantify your woes and enumerate possible remedies.
7. Quarry the facts by careful inquiry.
8. Quarter your troops in a back lot and go forward alone so the dialogue may begin.
9. Quash your impulse to run from the room.
10. Quell your own and others' fears about change.
11. Quench your thirst first with mineral water rather than spirits.
12. Query your motives before you express doubt about others' views.
13. Question the participants or adversaries in a conflict about what is going on.
14. Quibble only about what matters, not about minor points of grammar.
15. Quicken your step as you approach the unknown.
16. Quiet yourself before you seek information from others.
17. Quip often.
18. Quit trying to be a hero, and quit trying to make everything better.
19. Quiver only in the face of your own intelligent self-reflection.
20. Quiz others, while simultaneously keeping written documentation.
21. Quote the rules and describe the institution's behavioral norms.

Rest

Any effort you put toward self-care will be significant because you gain stamina and greater peace from it.

I AM DEEPLY COMMITTED to the life of the body. I listen to my spine, to my limbs and joints, to the totality of sensation. I welcome both stillness and movement. Many of us share these values; we appreciate our physicality and love to move and exert ourselves. The body is our source and resource for work. Ultimately, the body is an instrument of knowledge. The body is, of course, an expression of nature and natural processes. Its limitations affect everything we do, and many of us encounter those limitations daily. Though we live in a culture of body denial and abuse, the body ultimately asserts itself, demanding attention through pain or discomfort. Never mind that you are working diligently on the leadership path, aging, illness, and death are inevitable.

For Greek philosophers such as Aristotle, work was to be done in order to facilitate being at leisure. From the early Christian church fathers to Augustine, writers referred to holy leisure as *otium sanctum*, which means creating balance in life, an ability to be at peace throughout the activities of each day. Augustine saw the purpose of leisure as the pursuit of knowledge and truth. Later, monastic life was built on the concept of the *via contemplativa*, the way of contemplation and leisure. Like the Jewish Sabbath day, *otium* is not a three-minute break between activities, but a deeper spiritual rest that fosters peace and contentment.

Therefore, in the midst of life's demands find time for such *otium sanctum*. Readjust your expectations about what is reasonable, and recognize when you are tired and need to rest. Remember what has worked for you in the past, and reorganize your time to allow for these activities. It is permitted to rest from labor. Rest in nature. Rest at night.

MEDITATIONS ON DICHOTOMY

Why am I so stuck on the horns of responsibility?
Or,
why do I feel so obligated, and to whom?
I mean, to whom should I feel this obligation?
If not to myself, then to what or whom?

Why do I think I have *to do* and be of service to some greater cause?
Or,
why is it not enough *to be* in the morning, the day, the night?
I mean, why can't I sleep?
Why don't I sleep well?

Why can't I be content to do one thing and do it well?
Or,
why do I agonize about being of service to others?
I mean, why is enough never enough?

Why am I pulled in these two directions?
Or,
why does my longing wrestle with my responsibility?

I mean, why does this question grip me like no other?

Will it ever release me?
Or,
will I ever release it?

A PRESCRIPTION

One part solitude
Two parts relaxation with family and friends
Three parts massage
Four parts creative activity—writing, music, dance or art
Five parts meditation—of some sort
Six parts healing arts
Seven parts exercise
        and eight parts sleep.

Spirituality

Whatever your proclivity, nurture your inner life.

WE ARE BODY, MIND, *and* spirit. We know, or think we know, the body, but where is the mind? Where does the spirit reside? Both mind and spirit are incorporeal, ineffable, and rather mysterious, yet both are intricately related to breath. We can circle around them, as a pup circles his bed before lying down. But just as a dog must eventually lie down, we must rest ourselves in inner experience. And when we experience deeply, allowing ourselves to go off the road and into the woods, we often find that there are no words to capture what is so numinous. One must go deep before reaching the truly ineffable.

The word spirituality is derived from the Latin *spiritus,* "spirit" or "breath." The breath, like the spirit, is integral to life. Practices such as Christian centering prayer, Muslim prostrations, and Buddhist breath meditation rely on softening and synchronizing the breath with words, body movements, and awareness itself. Try this now. Inhale, count 1, 2, 3, 4. Hold the breath, 1, 2, 3, 4, 5, 6, 7. Exhale, 1, 2, 3, 4, 5, 6, 7, 8. Do this once, or more than once. Practice when you are upset and before you say anything to anyone. Practice before you sleep or when you awaken. Working with the breath soothes the nervous system.

And *spirituality*? What a tough word. My use of the word in this book is meant as a reminder to look within as you navigate your leadership path. The focus here is not religion per se, neither religious dogmas nor specific belief systems. Certainly, one's spiritual life may be directed within a particular religious tradition that involves prayer, meditation, study of sacred texts, and the like. But in my view, spirituality transcends these forms. Diverse cultures around the world express their spirituality in unique ways. Communities share forms of spiritual practice related to ritual performance and architecture, unifying time and place in the expression of key values. Spiritual practices are public, collective, and shared, as well as private, individual, and solitary. Through these disciplines we reach out, toward the world, and in, toward the self. I believe that one's spirituality and inner life must be *embodied*. We walk, run, dance, or sing. We practice yoga, tai chi, or martial arts. We cook or sit in nature. These are but a few examples of daily activities through which we can experience the profound interdependence of body, mind, and spirit.

As a leader, I have become attentive to how daily life itself may be considered a spiritual practice. Is it possible to overcome the separation of worldly and spiritual life through seeing daily life, including being in workplace, as a practice of awareness, mindfulness, and compassion? In daily life, we develop presence of mind. In daily life, we embody moral principles in acting on behalf of others. These, I believe, are the foundations of spirituality.

FROM THE CHRONICLES OF EXPERIENCE

I was raised in a secular household, with a Catholic mother and a Protestant father who could not agree upon the appropriate religious education for me and my sisters. My mother took us to many different churches during childhood, but always as visitors, never as participants in the ritual life of those communities. As a young child, I once asked her if she believed in God. She was thoughtful, then replied, "I believe in Mother Earth." Her comment was my introduction to a pantheistic worldview that sees all of nature as holy and sacred, and this has remained the root of my spiritual life ever since. I took a college course in world religions, but this was only a brief overview of the diversity of religious traditions.

My formal introduction to spirituality within the wisdom traditions came in my mid-twenties when I moved to the Lindisfarne Association, an educational community founded by William Irwin Thompson in the 1970s. There, I learned about Soto Zen Buddhism and sat zazen. I studied Sufi practices of prayer and dance, and practiced yoga in the lineage of B. K. S. Iyengar. During a trip to India to study at the Iyengar Yoga Institute, I stayed with a Parsi family in Mumbai, which triggered intense curiosity about Zoroastrian beliefs and spiritual practices. Attending a concert of singer Firoz Dastur with the family reminded me that music is a sacred art. Later, these experiences came to fruition in my studies of culture, philosophy, and religion at Harvard Divinity School and Harvard University.

As an adult, I visited Christian churches and joined in the rituals of the church year with friends and family. I became close to a rabbi who took me to temple and taught me what the Sabbath means. Participating in two Unitarian-Universalist communities in Idaho and Massachusetts offered opportunities to connect my spiritual values with social activism. I studied Indian philosophy and yoga in India, the US, and in England, then practiced and taught yoga for many years. I learned Zen, Theravadan, and Vajrayana forms of Buddhist meditation, and became a formal Buddhist practitioner in a community with a traditional Tibetan teacher.

My inner life has deepened during my years as a leader and administrator. This has been a multidimensional process with many spiritual insights. Here, I would share four directions of my reflection that are most pertinent to leadership. First, understanding the interconnectedness of all things has helped me to see both joyful and difficult situations as the result of causes and conditions, some of which I participated in creating, others with origins before I came onto the scene. Second, knowing that all actions of body, speech, and mind have consequences has made me less reactive and more patient with myself and others. Third, I aspire to embrace the great mysteries of birth, life, and death. This conviction that we live in a context of mystery makes me less certain that I am right and more prone to be open to my colleagues' ideas. Understanding that all human beings suffer has made me more compassionate, even toward adversaries.

The fourth direction of my musing concerns the complex question of how one conceptualizes the ultimate. What guides us as we traverse the path from birth to death, where leading others may have a significant role? What provides orientation for the many choices of daily life? Within various spiritual traditions, this ultimate point of reference has many names: Yahweh, God, or Allah; T'ien or Tao; Brahman, Nirvana, or Emptiness; Creativity, Nature, or Earth. Even those of us who are totally secular atheists orient our lives according to particular values and a vision of what life means. To bring mindful reflection about beliefs and action into daily life is the core of spirituality. I commend to you reflection about such matters.

Time

Time is cyclical, as every woman knows, but we also think of it as
linear, teleological, and eschatological. Time may be fast, or slow.
Like place, time shapes us even if we
do not have time to reflect about it.

PRACTICAL MATTERS FIRST. MANAGING one's time effectively is perhaps the
most difficult thing to learn while engaging in the ongoing demands of
leadership. Here are a few useful tips gleaned from my experience:

1. Write and answer email during one major session each day. Be careful not to spend all of your time simply responding to your inbox.
   This applies especially to those colleagues who will inundate you
   with email requests and demands. Sometimes I just file those in a
   special folder that I label "keep in case."

2. Make "to do" lists on a regular basis, daily or weekly as needed. The fifteenth-century Italian architect and author Leon Battista Alberti noted, "When I get up in the morning, before anything else I ask myself what I must do that day. These many things, I list them, I think about them, and assign to them the proper time...."[24]

3. In our era of speed, continuously interrupted attention, and fragmentation, we often feel we have no time to think. Synchronous with the production of extraordinary tools for investigating the world and ourselves, we are losing time for being and looking, as well as thinking.[25] Reserve time each day for both office work and for contemplation. Deep reflection cannot be hurried, and authentic leadership is based on insights that arise from such mindful thought.

4. Decide how much you want to be available for appointments and how long those appointments should be, but keep open drop-in hours that allow for the unknown and unexpected to walk through the door.

5. Consider the concept of *tempo giusto*, the right speed, which comes from the work of composers, musicians, and conductors seeking to establish the appropriate tempo for classical music.[26] The proponents of this view insist that most pre-classical and classical music should be played at half the speed of contemporary performances. What if we eschewed the more-better-faster mentality of today and conducted our own lives at half the speed demanded by our mobile devices?

6. Feminist philosopher Mary Daly gave the name "Clockocracy" to our society, which is ruled by clocks and calendars.[27] Could we set aside time for *otium*, rest, for getting away from the tyranny of the wristwatch and schedule?

METAPHORIC DIGRESSION: TIME AND MĀYĀ

Time is the matrix within which human life has meaning. But understanding what this meaning is, and how time and history figure in the process of creating or perceiving meaning, are mysterious and complex inquiries. In his short essay, "An Emerson Mood," Stanley Cavell stated that philosophical thinking about philosophical questions is not something one can submit to all the time, or at any time one might choose.[28] Once they come alive, such questions cannot be put aside like normal everyday questions. So it is for me in relation to time. Despairing about current world events, the pervasiveness of violence, and our seemingly unremitting race towards species annihilation, I wonder how best to understand time or the movement of history.

The Christian view of history, which dominates contemporary Western cultures, is that time is a directed movement with a beginning and an end, an ultimate fulfillment. The historical process is salvific. That is, in the temporal world where good and evil forces battle, salvation comes through history. History will end, but human life ends with resurrection into a better reality. Time also has a center. For the Christian, this is the birth, life, and death of Jesus. And a monotheistic God figures as the "lord of time" who controls the universal history of humankind.

For some theologians, the Jewish prophetic and Christian apocalyptic interpretations of history are combined in the biblical Revelation of John, where the victory of the forces of good occurs in a world catastrophe. In my view, this combination of teleological and eschatological views of time has been disastrous, in that it has shaped many evangelical and ecclesiastical movements during the past few millennia. Such expectations also undergird the glibness of military and governmental leaders when they derail attempts to end nuclear weapons testing, refuse to participate in talks aimed at establishing peace in war torn areas of the world, or deny that global warming and climate change are underway.

By contrast, I am fascinated by the views of time that evolved within Hindu mythology and philosophy, particularly in Puranic texts that were written down between 1000 BCE and 600 CE. There, time is seen as a cyclical process organized around several distinct principles, including the *yugas* and *māyā*. These principles are outlined in countless stories about gods and goddesses of the Hindu pantheon. The *yugas*, or world cycles, describe the creation, life, and destruction of the world through four distinct ages. We live in the fourth and last *Kali yuga*, a time of strife, quarrels, and war. In this *yuga*, both humans and the world are at their worst, and the world will ultimately dissolve in order for another world cycle to begin. Within this view, good does not increase as change occurs, but value lies in repetition and sameness. The *yugas*, along with the yearly calendar, are part of the cyclical process of *kala* or time. And *kala* unfolds in and through *māyā*.

Māyā, like time in general, is a complex concept. In early Vedic litera-ture, *māyā* indicates the power of the gods, as well as devices of deception used by demons. By the time of the Upanishads, *māyā* was no longer the exclusive domain of the gods and demons, but it meant energy or strength, and it was associated with change itself. The word was used in these texts in many different ways: as cosmic illusion, duality, magic, or simply power and energy. In Hindu literary epics, *māyā* was associated with the idea of illusion. And later, in Advaita philosophy, it was understood as a form of cosmic illusion that veils truth. In the Puranas, many of these definitions were used. On the one hand, *māyā* deludes and draws us into the imper-manent world that we mistakenly view as permanent; on the other, it is creative energy itself, embodied *in* the world. *Māyā* is clearly an ongoing generative force in the cosmos.

The understanding of time as cyclical and generative, with a strange illusory quality, seems to be grounded in human sensory experience, in the human body, and especially in the experience of being an embodied self. Linear, progressive time seems to be based on imagination and thought, on the capacity to remember and to fantasize. In short, it is based on the activi-ties of mind alone. Human life—my life, your life—happens in a matrix of time, perceived experientially and viscerally, and understood intellectually. For me, the Indian concept of *māyā* adds the insight that this time matrix is both illusory and creative. Traversing your leadership path, study your own view of time. Understand that, like a plant, you will grow and develop through the seasons of your job. This natural process reflects the multiple dimensions of time, and it takes time. Be patient.

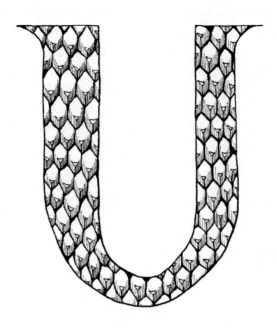

Universe

To invoke the universe is to bring your attention
to The Big Picture.

HOW DOES ONE NAME the most encompassing sense of all that is? We might speak of the universe or the cosmos. While "universe" takes us immediately to astronomical speculations about galaxies, space travel, and intelligent life elsewhere, "cosmology" conjures myths of ancient beginnings and future fates. Within Chinese Taoist and Japanese Zen Buddhist traditions, "ten thousand things" is given to this idea of limitless phenomena in the universe. I recently read *Ten Thousand Joys and Ten Thousand Sorrows*, an exceptional narrative by Olivia Ames Hoblitzelle about her husband's descent into Alzheimer's disease. The book was a reminder that "ten thousand things" encompasses all of life, including aging and dying.

With notions of "great time" and "small time," Russian philosopher Mikhail Bakhtin used temporal metaphors to talk about the relationship of The Big Picture to everyday life. Bakhtin's ideas have had a great impact on me over several decades, and I often muse about this distinction. An act considered in small time, for instance, would be examined in relation to its present context, as well as the recent past and immediate future. The category of great time is more useful for understanding nations and cultures. Great time means the "infinite and unfinalized dialogue in which no meaning dies," he wrote in a set of notes in 1971, shortly before he died.[29]

Most of us on the leadership path live and work in small time, with the occasional sense that our actions belong to a longer trajectory. My participation in building a new arts facility slips, at least in my imagination, into great time because I imagine future generations creating in its spaces.

In Greek philosophy, the antithesis of such optimistic images is articulated in Plato's famous allegory of the cave, from Book VII of *The Republic*. In this narrative, prisoners sit on the ground, shackled, and watch the play of shadows on the wall in front of them. Behind them a fire burns, while puppeteers walk across a parapet, creating a display of light and shadow that the prisoners assume to be real objects and events. There is more to this allegory, related to the Platonic theory of forms, but I have always found it an apt description of how most of us lead our lives. Caught up by the interplay of shadowy projections in the mind and never turning around to leave our caves for the actual world outside, we live truncated lives.

A wise leader will make every effort to keep the biggest possible perspective on the nitty-gritty details of daily experience.

Vision

Vision does not equal seeing. Vision is physical sight
and perceptual processes plus imagination.

WHAT DRIVES US AS leaders in our communities? How do we balance the
need to offer our gifts, skills, and vision to the world and its diverse institutions, along with the need for recognition and affirmation? And who
among us does not devote much of daily life to our ever-present computer,
television, and mobile screens? My vision needs nature, seeing the colors
of the world, especially the palette of greens and yellows that emerge first
in the spring garden, or in winter, the prismatic sparkles caused when sun
rises on fresh snow. I must stretch my eyes, literally, to use my distance
vision, to find the distant horizon.

I was impressed when I first came to my present institution that there was no shared vision in my department. I had the immediate impression that there was little focus and no obvious way to unify my colleagues to act for particular goals. In time, our new building became an effective rallying point, but such a grand possibility is not the only way to develop a vision. A vision can be personal *and* collective. Cultivate your private vision about the direction of your organization, then work with colleagues to help shape a collective vision and work toward shared goals.

Certainly, you will spend much time focused on the practical day-to-day work of running your department, committee, institution, or company. But keep your gaze on both your own and the organization's future, what I call "the long horizon." In the midst of the process of articulating your vision, undertake processes of self-care. Much has been written about how to do this. But more than anything else, finding moments, evenings, and days of silence will nourish your stamina and your spirit for the demanding work of serving as a leader. Eye exercises, such as those described in the mindfulness chapter, can be helpful for the body. And it is useful to remember that if you move too close to a mirror, you don't get a very good sense of yourself! Some goals take a long time to come to fruition and will very likely evolve after your time in the leadership position is over. Remember the adage that we learn more through our failures than from our successes.

METAPHORIC DIGRESSION: CRYING FOR A VISION

I borrow this expressive title from David Michael Levin's book *The Opening of Vision*.[30] Our eyes not only serve as organs of sight, but are also emotionally expressive. Only human beings cook and cry and analyze our experiences. Levin asks us to consider what each of us has seen in our lifetime and to consider what other generations saw. We, our ancestors, and those we will never know, have suffered. We have seen horrors—violence, hatred, and injustice. And what we have seen, even indirectly through others' eyes, calls to us. Our seeing calls for a response that may bring tears. Simultaneously, we may see the inadequacy of our visionary power—the inability to sense the proportions of the responsibility each of us bears for the reality of what is seen. Questions arise as I write, Mr. Levin whispering in my ear.

What *is* crying?

Is it only an accident that our eyes are organs of both sight and crying, of vision and tears? Is there a relationship, perhaps even an intimate relationship, between them?

Is crying essential for and to vision?

Might crying be a mode of visionary being or visionary imagination?

Although crying is involuntary, what would happen if we took it up as a mindfulness practice? Such a practice would be concerned with cultivating our capacity for care, for feeling and vision itself. When that vision begins to make a difference in the world and gathers others into its wisdom, crying becomes a critical practice of the self. Crying arises from human needs for contact, wholeness, and openness, all of which arise not just from the ego, but from the inner self. Through the eyes, we make contact with things and persons around us, and we cry when that vision breaks down. But we need wholeness and the capacity to see more of *what is* in this historical moment. Most of us do not recognize this need, either in ourselves or in the world in which we live. We may experience psychic numbing, the inability to feel at all. In the present context, crying may be an appropriate response.

"Crying is the rooting of vision in the world," Levin admonishes us.[31] Insight is the result of entering mindfully into this practice of grounding our vision in the world as it presents itself, and insight can become the foundation for new understanding and new vision. Lest I be misunderstood here, I am not talking only about literal crying. I was so taken by Levin's image of "crying for a vision" because crying and tears can also be understood as a process involving awareness, imagination, and thought.

In his *Notebooks*, written between 1935 and 1951, Albert Camus famously wrote that we should live to the point of tears.[32] What happens when we *imagine* these tears? When we think, and understand, that tears are an appropriate response to something? Such experiences can lead the leader of others to a more profound sense of direction and vision.

Wisdom

Cultivating wisdom on the leadership path is a path in itself.

Wisdom is not clever opinion, but humility as we face the mysteries of birth, illness, aging, and death. Wisdom comes from experiencing joy as well as pain. And to some extent, it comes from experiencing joy regardless of whatever else is happening. We all have what it takes to generate wisdom, if we would but follow our path with awareness and self-reflection. The basic instructions are simple: Develop and trust your own experiential knowledge. Live with a good heart. Cultivate kindness toward others and engage in selfless service for the common good. Prepare for death. For me, this last is life's greatest mystery and challenge. It is hard to cultivate nonattachment to the impermanent things of this life—to individuals, possessions, wealth, fame, and the like. But knowing deeply that all things must die leads to the decision to cultivate wisdom.

A *decision* to cultivate wisdom, you might ask? Where does wisdom come from? How do we know it when we see it? And how is wisdom a path in itself?

METAPHORIC DIGRESSION: WISDOM TRADITIONS

The insight and intelligence of the human race are collected in the world's wisdom traditions, which are "data banks" of human wisdom, though not everything in them is wise.[33] From Aldous Huxley and E. F. Schumacher to Huston Smith, wise individuals have encouraged us to consult and profit from the ethics, virtues, and vision of what Huxley called "perennial philosophy." Other wise ones—theologian Mary Daly and activist Starhawk come to mind—urge us to beware of the cultural baggage, social mores, and outdated cosmologies that also characterize these traditions. We live in a world of religious pluralism and diversity, expressed in both individual and cultural forms. Listening to others and seeking to understand their worldviews is absolutely crucial when we undertake the responsibilities of leadership.

Because I did not have a religious education as a child, I turned first to philosophy when I began my search to understand the meaning of life. I learned that we must create our own meaning from Albert Camus, Jean-Paul Sartre, Simone de Beauvoir, and other existentialists. Like them, I was fascinated by the way anxiety, a sense of nothingness, and awareness of death shaped my young life. Later, as a result of making art, I was drawn to investigate comparative mythology and ritual. A sincere interest in the wisdom traditions of Asia grew from studying art history. By the time I began my graduate studies in religion and art history at Harvard, the biggest lacuna in my education concerned the Abrahamic religions—Christianity, Judaism, and Islam.

I studied for seven years with the theologian Gordon D. Kaufman (1925–2011), whose understanding of Christian theology as imaginative construction focused on theology as an open and evolving discourse, rather than as a set of revealed and tradition-bound doctrines. Such imaginative construction helps us to articulate our place within the cosmos. In his many books and articles, Kaufman argued that traditional views of the theological task are misleading because they fail to articulate the fundamental role of imagination in the process of analysis, criticism, and reconstruction of categories such as God and Jesus, humanity and world.[34]

Kaufman dedicated much of his life to looking at how the concept of God functions in our language and experience. Reification, the process of mistaking our symbols as having concrete or material existence in reality, is a dangerous tendency in faith-based religious writing. Instead of understanding the word "God" as referring to a process related to reality but essentially mysterious, theologians, interpreters of scripture, and laypeople have mistakenly understood God in reified form: as supernatural being, powerful ego, father, king, and lord over all.

Up until the time of his death, Kaufman also engaged in interreligious dialogue, especially among Christians and Buddhists. As a way of setting up a conversation between "God" and "emptiness," for example, Kaufman described each of these concepts as a way of naming ultimate reality. But as Rita Gross so vividly described in her published dialogue with him, Buddhist views of ultimate reality are experiential, not conceptual. They are non-dual, not separate from *things as they are* in this present moment. Ultimate reality is not "this and that," like the concept of God. Instead, it is "just this," the experience of the present moment.[35] While emptiness is a central concept in Buddhist worldviews, it does not function in the same way as the concept of God does for Christians.

The word "emptiness" articulates a profound yet difficult-to-grasp idea that is easily misunderstood. It means, simply, that nothing has or carries intrinsic existence. Everything in the universe—persons, events, nature itself—originates through codependent causes and conditions. Every life is the result of thoroughly interrelated conditions that give rise to the uniqueness of that life's expression in each moment. The same principle applies to the self. There *is* no singular, permanent, intrinsic self. All aspects of the self, including the body, one's experience, and thought itself, arise through interdependent processes. I have "no self" in the sense that every aspect of my being came about and continues to evolve through processes involving other persons within the natural and created worlds. Emptiness, as Rita Gross described this term, must be linked to *suchness*, the "just this" mentioned above. "On the one hand, because everything is empty, then everything is sacred. On the other hand, because everything is empty, nothing is fixed or solid."[36] There is no reified absolute other or ultimate reality in this worldview, but *this* reality is nevertheless sacred, fluid, and luminous.

Understanding similarities and differences in the wisdom traditions has had a profound impact on my experience as a leader of others. My years of study with Gordon Kaufman led me to the conviction that all of the world's philosophies and religions are constructions of the human imagination. Knowing this, they continue to provide orientation for myself and others. You may find it advantageous to acknowledge that imagination is a powerful force in all human interactions. Even a beginner's understanding of Buddhist philosophy, especially the concepts of impermanence and emptiness, can influence your reactions in situations of difficulty. Ultimately, the wisdom of these traditions is expressed in ethics and a vision of reality. In terms of an ethical stance, the biblical Decalogue tells it all, as Huston Smith noted.[37] Murder, theft, lying, stealing, and sexual misconduct are all to be avoided. Practicing virtues of humility and selflessness, of charity and compassion, and of seeking truth(s) can help us to lead others effectively.

We do not invent wisdom, for it is all around us if we proceed on life's paths, and the leadership path in particular, with our eyes wide open. We know it when there is deep resonance between ideas and felt experience. We know it when we allow the wisdom of others and our own cultural traditions to impact our thinking, feeling, and acting.

I lived for many years in the Pacific Northwest, where the wisdom—and pain—of Indian tribes such as the Duwamish, Suquamish, and Nez Perce were part of my education. These native people endured tremendous hardship, suffering, and cultural annihilation, yet their wisdom traditions also have profound resilience. When I moved to Colorado, I investigated native traditions in this region, tracing the history of Chief Niwot's band of Southern Arapaho, most of whom were murdered in the Sand Creek Massacre that occurred in 1864, less than one hundred miles from where I currently live. Farther south, the Navajo fared little better. In 1863 their crops and homes were destroyed on orders from the U.S. government. Following the catastrophic Long Walk, a three hundred-mile journey to Fort Sumner in New Mexico where they were put in a camp, they were returned to a mere 24,000 square miles of government allotted land.

The Navajo worldview sees the human being as totally interrelated within the environmental context. Everything exists in dualities, which belong together and balance each other. This equilibrium and harmony can be broken in numerous ways, and symptoms of illness mean that balance must be restored. Therefore, Navajo life is traditionally governed by complex rules that serve to maintain harmony. One well-known form for restoring balance is the Beauty Way Chant, which can be found in numerous print and online versions. Acknowledging that the possibility of healing, of *beauty*, exists everywhere—especially before, behind, above, and below me—I endeavor to walk in beauty. Restoring balance and harmony in my relations with others, with nature, and the wider world, I can then honestly say "It is finished in beauty."[38] To me, this chant, even excised from its ritual context, epitomizes the idea that wisdom is a path in itself.

Xenophobia

Smile at the unknown as you come to terms with reality.

THOUGH OFTEN REFERRED TO as fear of strangers, xenophobia is actually a more general term that derives from the Greek *xenos* (alien, foreign, or strange) and *phobia* (fear). Perhaps the most dysfunctional and limiting quality that we can bring into positions of leadership is fear of the unknown. The capacity to welcome the unfamiliar and to be comfortable with uncertainty is to see the unknown as a potential arena for individual growth. And what is reality, anyway? We often respond to everyday life habitually, in familiar ways. But habits may blind us to what is really going on. Based on values of openness and equanimity, we would do well to cultivate love of the unknown or *xenophilia* instead.

I do not mean to be glib here, for fear is a fundamental human emotion. Some fears are well-founded. However, we would be wise to face insecurities about our own identity, alter any feeling that the universe is a hostile place, and release the belief that only "I" can make things happen. We would also be wise to face the shadow side of our personality, especially as it manifests in fear of the unknown and denial of death.

Parker Palmer has described how fear is one of the most common and longstanding human responses to experience. It originated in struggles to overcome ancient enemies, including animals, other humans, and even darkness. The maxim "be not afraid" is common to all of the world's wisdom traditions, but it does not mean that we will never be afraid. As Palmer puts it, "We do not have to *be* the fear we have. We do not have to lead from a place of fear, thereby engendering a world in which fear is multiplied."[39] How do we accomplish this transformation? By cultivating self-awareness, by finding mentors and confidantes with whom to talk about thoughts and feelings, anxieties and fears, and by fostering faith and trust that it *is* possible to change habitual modes of thought and ways of acting.

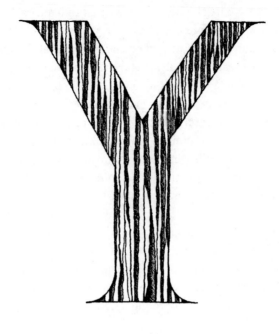

Yesterday

In several of his fragments, the Greek philosopher Herakleitos ruminated about time, change, and the past. He reminds us that "one cannot step twice into the same river, for the water into which you first stepped has flowed on."[40]

IN DEALING WITH THE past, be self-effacing and humble. Don't rise to being baited by colleagues, but tell them the past is over. Try focusing on the present as it moves toward the future. You will be able to help others when you are able to communicate how you released your own desire to hold onto the past.

I once had a colleague whose primary *modus operandi* involved complaints, angry accusations, and extreme bullying. I experienced this personally dozens of times, and I knew from others that this person had caused them tremendous pain. My responses ran the gamut from deep listening, understanding, and impatience, to making efforts to thwart her. Sometimes in our interactions I was genuinely constructive, but I also made mistakes. Then, I had an extraordinary dream: we were walking together outdoors, arm in arm, like sisters. This dream had a tremendous impact on both my feelings about her and consideration of how best to engage her. She did not cease acting in ways that demeaned or hurt others. My own diverse reactions did not suddenly stop. But I began to forgive myself for those times when I had erred. I also began to develop a fragile compassion for her, and later, a genuine wish that she might be happy. If I had held onto a narrow view of our individual and shared pasts, I would never have been able to grow, to develop new responses, and ultimately, to be fully in the present with her. By the time she retired, I felt more at ease with her. Even though I attempted to communicate the transformation of my own feelings, she remained angry with me. And this taught me, again, that we are not responsible for others' tendencies to hold on to the past. Understanding the deep humanity of all persons, you can begin to cultivate forgiveness for your own and others' past transgressions.

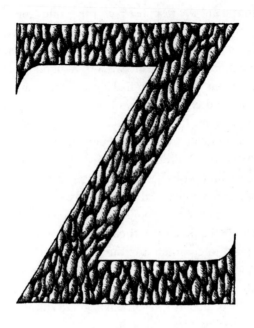

Zipper

One of the fundamental lessons for a person on the leadership
path concerns when to use the zipper most effectively—
particularly when to "zip it"!

LEADERS OFTEN FEEL THAT they must speak on every issue that comes before them or that faces the group they lead. If I always speak, my colleagues
may become dependent on me, waiting to hear what I think before thinking for themselves. Often, the right move is to encourage others to speak,
thereby allowing the group to build its own capacity for self-governance by
hashing out the issues at hand. Some leaders are great talkers, even charis-
matic, and enjoy the attention and ego-gratification this brings. But if you
understand the concept of the servant-leader that undergirds this book,
you will consciously consider the virtues of silence.

METAPHORIC DIGRESSION: THE ZIPPER, AN ASSAY[41]

Then

I created my first hand-bound book when I was six years old, an "ABC" that began with Apple and ended with Zipper. I didn't know that "zip" was first used in English in the 1850s, or that the word refers to the sound made by a rapidly moving object.

In 1851 Elias Howe purchased a patent for an Automatic Continuous Clothing Closure, which he never developed. Nearly four decades later, Whitcomb Judson patented a Clasp Locker and displayed it at the 1893 Chicago World's Fair. The first Parliament of World Religions occurred simultaneously in Chicago, but we do not know if any of the attendees saw Judson's Locker. In 1913 Gideon Sundback tried to improve upon the Judson C-curity and created his Separable Fastener. In 1925 B. F. Goodrich registered "Zipper Boots" and added zippers to popular tobacco pouches. Their efforts to trademark the word zipper ultimately failed. In the 1930s manufacturers of children's clothing began using this device, marketed to increase a child's self-reliance. Later in the 30s, French designers sewed zippers into men's trousers, where their popularity beat the button.

The rest is fashion history.

Now

Take a close look at the zippers in your life: on jackets and handbags, trousers and shoes, children's clothing, suitcases and backpacks. These handy devices share a fundamental characteristic: they keep what is meant to be inside *inside*.

Epilogue

TRADITIONALLY, AN EPILOGUE AT the end of a literary work deals with the future of its characters. In a few lines titled "Three Wisdoms," M. C. Richards described characters who reflect three distinctive styles of living: "Go slow," said the snail. "Hop! Hop!" said the hare. "Pace yourself," said the cheetah, "it's a long run."[42]

What will your leadership path look like?
How will it grow and how will you nurture it?
How will your inner work be reflected in your outer public life?

You, the reader, are the main character here. So, the final word is yours.

Endnotes

A

1. Bakhtin, *Toward a Philosophy of the Act*, 3.

B

2. Compare, for instance, the translations of Patrick, http://www.classic persuasion.org/pw/heraclitus/herpate.htm, fragment 70; Kirk, *Heraclitus: The Cosmic Fragments*, fragment 103, p. 113; Davenport, *Herakleitos*, fragment 109, p. 29; and Haxton, *Fragments*, fragment 70, p. 45.

3. This is a paraphrase of a remark made by poet Jane Hirshfield in San Francisco on November 18, 2011, at the national conference of the American Academy of Religion.

C

4. Developed as a theme throughout Saiving, "Human Situation."

5. Hirshfield, in Gregory and Mrozick, eds., *Women Practicing Buddhism*, 46.

D

6. See http://one.laptop.org/about/mission for further information on this project.

7. Haraway, "Manifesto for Cyborgs," 203–4.

8. See Haynes, "On the Need for Ethical Aesthetics," 75–82.

H

9. I owe my reflections about hope as a memory of the future to a chapter in philosopher Gabriel Marcel's *Homo Viator*. I explored these and related ideas about creativity and utopia in my 1997 *Vocation of the Artist*.

I

10. Rinpoche, *Words*, 59.

11. See Winnicott, *The Family*, 1965, as well as his later books and articles.
12. Rosenberg, *Living in the Light of Death*, esp. 87–107.
13. Hall, *Lifework*, 62.

K

14. I especially thank Sharon Welch, distinguished leader, writer, and teacher, for introducing me to Beard's delightful recipe, and for embodying the interconnection of physical and intellectual nurturance that I emphasize here.

L

15. Hunt, *Afterlife of Gardens*, passim.
16. Gary Snyder's reflections on path in *Practice of the Wild* have been enormously helpful to me in reflecting about leadership. Here he is quoting Dogen. See especially pp. 9–10, 145–54.
17. These are adapted from Larry Spears and his collaborators in *Practicing Servant-Leadership*, esp. Ch. 2 by Warren Bennis.

M

18. I learned these practices from dancer, teacher, and leader Barbara Dilley. Dilley originally introduced them in a 1996 public performance titled *Naked Face*, performed at the Boulder Museum of Contemporary Art by the Mariposa Collective and directed by her.

N

19. Calvino, *Six Memos*, 124.

P

20. No one has written more clearly about place than Edward Casey in his many books on the subject, and I am indebted to his systematic reflections.

Q

21. For more information on CDR, see http://www.mediate.org/.
22. I especially thank Darci Meyer and Andrew Holocek for their skilled teaching on this topic.
23. Carl Rogers' writing is accessible in many books and articles. For an often-reprinted article that is pertinent to communication styles, leadership, and business, see Rogers and Roethlisberger, "Barriers and Gateways."

T

24. Quoted in Honoré, *In Praise of Slowness*, 23.
25. See Levy, "No Time to Think," 237–49.
26. See http://www.tempogiusto.de for more on this development.
27. Daly, *Webster's First New Intergalactic Wickedary*, 279.
28. Cavell, *Emerson's Transcendental Etudes*, 26.

U

29. Bakhtin, *Speech Genres*, 169.

V

30. Levin, *Opening of Vision*, esp. pp. 170–91.
31. Levin, *Opening of Vision*, 191.
32. Camus, *Notebooks*, 51

W

33. Smith, *World's Religions*, 5.
34. See Kaufman, *In Face of Mystery*, for the most comprehensive statement of his theology.
35. Gross, "This Is It," 189.
36. Ibid., 196.
37. Smith, *World's Religions*, 387.
38. See Keeney, *Walking Thunder*, 161. This book contains a fine rendering of the full chant in English, as well as a CD of Walking Thunder, a Diné (Navajo) medicine woman, reciting in her native language.

X

39. Palmer, *Let Your Life Speak*, 93–94.

Y

40. Davenport, *Herakleitos*, 14.

Z

41. I offer this reflection in homage to poet Jane Hirshfield, who has published a number of poems using "assay" in the title. An assay is an analysis, a process whose name derives from biology, pharmacology, and medicine.

EPILOGUE

42. I heard Richards recite this many times, and it appears in print in her *Crossing Point*, 1.

Selected Resources

Adams, George, and Olive Whicher. *The Plant between Sun and Earth*. Boulder, CO: Shambhala, 1982.

Bakhtin, Mikhail M. *Speech Genres and Other Late Essays*. Edited by Caryl Emerson and Michael Holquist. Translated by Vern W. McGee. Austin: University of Texas Press, 1986.

———. *Toward a Philosophy of the Act*. Edited by Vadim Liapunov and Michael Holquist. Translated by Vadim Liapunov. Austin: University of Texas Press, 1993.

Baudrillard, Jean. *Simulacra and Simulation*. Translated by Sheila Faria Glaser. Ann Arbor: University of Michigan Press, 1994.

Calvino, Italo. *Six Memos for the Next Millenium*. New York: Vintage, 1988.

Camus, Albert. *Notebooks 1935–1951*. New York: Marlowe, 1998.

Casey, Edward. *The Fate of Place: A Philosophical History*. Berkeley: University of California Press, 1997.

———. *Getting Back into Place: Toward a Renewed Understanding of the Place-World*. Bloomington: Indiana University Press, 1993.

Cavell, Stanley. *Emerson's Transcendental Etudes*. Edited by David Justin Hodge. Stanford: Stanford University Press, 2003.

Chödrön, Pema. *Comfortable with Uncertainty*. Boston: Shambhala, 2002.

Cleary, Thomas, trans. *Zen Lessons: The Art of Leadership*. Boston: Shambhala, 1989.

Collins, James, and Jerry I. Porras. *Built to Last: Successful Habits of Visionary Companies*. NY: Harper Business, 1994.

Collins, James. *Good to Great: Why Some Companies Make the Leap—and Others Don't*. New York: Harper Business, 2001.

Covey, Stephen. *Living the Seven Habits: Applications and Insights*. Provo, UT: Covey Leadership Center, 1992.

Daly, Mary. *Websters' First New Intergalactic Wickedary of the English Language*. Conjured in Cahoots with Jane Caputi. Boston: Beacon, 1987.

Davenport, Guy, translator. *Herakleitos and Diogenes*. Bolinas, CA: Grey Fox, 1979.

DeLuca, Joel R. *Political Savvy: Systematic Approaches to Leadership behind the Scenes*. Berwyn, PA: Evergreen Business Group, 1999.

De Pree, Max. *Leadership Is an Art*. East Lansing: Michigan State University Press, 1987.

Eddy, Bill. *"It's All YOUR Fault: 12 Tips for Managing People Who Blame Others for Everything*. Santa Ana, CA: Janis, 2008.

Eliot, T. S. *Four Quartets*. New York: Harcourt, Brace, and World, 1942.

Fisher, Roger, and William Ury. *Getting to Yes*. Boston: Houghton Mifflin, 1981.

Forster, E. M. "The Machine Stops." In *The Eternal Moment*. New York: Harcourt, Brace, 1928. Available online: http://archive.ncsa.illinois.edu/prajlich/forster.html.

Foster, Richard. *Celebration of Discipline.* 3rd ed. San Francisco: HarperSanFrancisco, 1988.

Gardner, Howard. *Leading Minds, An Anatomy of Leadership.* New York: Basic Books, 1995.

Gendlin, Eugene T. *Focusing.* 2nd ed. New York: Bantam, 1981.

Greenleaf, Robert K. *Servant Leadership: A Journey into the Nature of Legitimate Power and Greatness.* New York: Paulist, 1977.

Gregory, Peter N. and Susanne Mrozick, editors. *Women Practicing Buddhism: American Experiences.* Boston: Wisdom Publications, 2008.

Gross, Rita M. "This Is It: Nothing Happens Next." *Buddhist-Christian Studies* 9 (1989) 189–212.

Hanh, Thich Nhat. *The Miracle of Mindfulness: A Manual of Meditation.* Translated by Mobi Warren. Boston: Beacon, 1976.

Haraway, Donna. "A Manifesto for Cyborgs." In *Feminism / Postmodernism*, edited by Linda J. Nicholson, 199–233. New York: Routledge, 1990.

Hart, Tobin. "Opening the Contemplative Mind in the Classroom." *Journal of Transformative Education* 2 (Jan 2004) 28–46.

Haxton, Brooks, trans. *Fragments: The Collected Wisdom of Heraclitus.* New York: Viking, 2001.

Haynes, Deborah J. *Art Lessons: Meditations on the Creative Life.* Boulder, CO: Westview, 2003.

———. *Book of This Place: The Land, Art, and Spirituality.* Eugene, OR: Pickwick Publications, 2009.

———. "On the Need for Ethical Aesthetics: Or, Where I Stand between Neo-Luddites and Cyberians." *Art Journal* 56 (Fall 1997) 75–82.

———. *The Vocation of the Artist.* New York: Cambridge University Press, 1997.

Hindle, Tim. *Manage Your Time.* New York: DK, 1998.

Hirshfield, Jane. *After: Poems.* New York: HarperCollins, 2006.

———. *Come, Thief: Poems.* New York: Knopf, 2011.

———. *Hiddenness, Uncertainty, Surprise: Three Generative Energies of Poetry.* Newcastle: Bloodaxe, 2008.

Hoblitzelle, Olivia Ames. *Ten Thousand Joys and Ten Thousand Sorrows.* Los Angeles: Tarcher/Penguin, 2010.

Honoré, Carl. *In Praise of Slowness: How a Worldwide Movement Is Challenging the Cult of Speed.* San Francisco: HarperSanFrancisco, 2004.

Hunt, John Dixon. *The Afterlife of Gardens.* Philadelphia: University of Pennsylvania Press, 2004.

Kaufman, Gordon D. *In Face of Mystery: A Constructive Theology.* Cambridge: Harvard University Press, 1993.

Keeney, Bradford, editor. *Walking Thunder: Diné Medicine Woman.* Philadelphia: Ringing Books, 2001.

Kirk, G. S., translator. *Heraclitus: The Cosmic Fragments.* Cambridge: Cambridge University Press, 1954.

Kolodny, Annette. *Failing the Future: A Dean Looks at Higher Education in the Twenty-first Century.* Durham: Duke University Press, 1998.

Lasater, Judith. *Living Your Yoga, Finding the Spiritual in Everyday Life.* Berkeley: Rodmell, 2000.

Levin, David Michael. *The Opening of Vision: Nihilism and the Postmodern Situation.* New York: Routledge, 1988.

Levy, David M. "No Time to Think: Reflections on Information Technology and Contemporary Scholarship." *Ethics and Information Technology* 9 (2007) 237–49.

Lister, Martin. *New Media: A Critical Introduction.* New York: Routledge, 2009.

Marcel, Gabriel. *Homo Viator: Introduction to a Metaphysic of Hope.* Translated by Emma Craufurd. Chicago: Regnery, 1951.

Mindel, Arnold. *The Leader as Martial Artist: An Introduction to Deep Democracy.* San Francisco: Harper, 1992.

Moore, Christopher W. *The Mediation Process: Practical Strategies for Resolving Conflict.* 2nd ed. San Francisco: Jossey-Bass, 1996.

Negroponte, Nicholas. *Being Digital.* New York: Knopf, 1995.

Palmer, Parker J. *Let Your Life Speak: Listening for the Voice of Vocation.* San Francisco: Jossey-Bass, 2000.

Patrick, G. T. W., translator. *The Fragments of the Work of Heraclitus of Ephesus on Nature.* Baltimore: Murray, 1889. Available online: http://www.classicpersuasion.org/pw/heraclitus/herpate.htm.

Patterson, Kerry et al. *Crucial Conversations: Tools for Talking When Stakes Are High.* 2nd ed. New York: McGraw-Hill, 2012.

Plato. *The Republic.* Translated by R. E. Allen. New Haven: Yale University Press, 2006.

Richards, Mary Caroline. *Centering in Pottery, Poetry, and the Person.* Middletown, CT: Wesleyan University Press, 1964.

———. *The Crossing Point: Selected Talks and Writings.* Middletown, CT: Wesleyan University Press, 1973.

———. *Opening Our Moral Eye: Essays, Talks & Poems Embracing Creativity & Community.* Edited by Deborah J. Haynes. Hudson, NY: Lindisfarne, 1996.

Rinpoche, Patrul. *The Words of My Perfect Teacher.* Translated by Padmakara Translation Group. Boston: Shambhala, 1998.

Rogers, Carl R., and F. J. Roethlisberger. "Barriers and Gateways to Communication." *Harvard Business Review* 69 (Nov/Dec 1991) 105–11.

Rosenberg, Larry, with David Guy. *Living in the Light of Death: On the Art of Being Fully Alive.* Boston: Shambhala, 2001.

Saiving, Valerie. "The Human Situation, A Feminine View." In *Womanspirit Rising: A Feminist Reader in Religion,* edited by Carol Christ and Judith Plaskow, 25–42. San Francisco: Harper & Row, 1979.

Schumacher, E. F. *A Guide for the Perplexed.* New York: Harper & Row, 1977.

Smith, Huston. *The World's Religions.* San Francisco: HarperSanFrancisco, 1991.

Snyder, Gary. *The Practice of the Wild.* San Francisco: North Point Press, 1990.

Spears, Larry C. and Michele Lawrence, editors. *Practicing Servant-Leadership: Succeeding through Trust, Bravery, and Forgiveness.* San Francisco: Jossey-Bass, 2004.

Starhawk. *Dreaming the Dark: Magic, Sex, and Politics.* Boston: Beacon, 1988.

Tucker, Allan. *Chairing the Academic Department: Leadership Among Peers.* Phoenix: Oryx, 1993.

Twale, Darla J., and Barbara M. De Luca. *Faculty Incivility: The Rise of the Academic Bully Culture and What To Do About It.* San Francisco: Jossey-Bass, 2008.

Welwood, John, editor. *Ordinary Magic: Everyday Life as Spiritual Path.* Boston: Shambhala, 1992.

Whicher, Olive. *Projective Geometry: Creative Polarities in Space and Time.* London: Steiner, 1971.

Winnicott, D. W. *The Family and Individual Development.* New York: Basic Books, 1965.

Index